Letters from the Country
IV

Letters from the Country
IV

Marsha Boulton

McArthur & Company

First printed in Canada by McArthur & Company, 2002

National Library of Canada Cataloguing in Publication Data

Boulton, Marsha
 Letters from the country IV

ISBN 1-55278-265-4

 1. Farm life—Ontario—Anecdotes. I. Title.

S522.C3B684 2002   630'.9713   C2002-900488-8

Composition and Design by *Michael P. Callaghan*
Typeset at *Moons of Jupiter*
Author Photograph by J*ohn Reeves*
Cover Design by *Tania Craan*
Printed in Canada by *Transcontinental Printing*

McArthur & Company
322 King Street West, Suite 402
Toronto, Ontario, M5V 1J2

The publisher would like to acknowledge the financial support of the
Government of Canada through the Book Publishing Industry
Development Program (BPIDP) and the Canada Council for our publishing activities. The publisher further wishes to acknowledge the
financial support of the Ontario Arts Council for our publishing program.

10 9 8 7 6 5 4 3 2 1

Table of Contents

❧❧❧❧❧❧

Spring

Summer

Autumn

Winter

Foreword and Acknowledgments

There is a subtle war going on between the country and the city. People who have lived in the country all of their lives are seeing "their" territory overrun by outsiders with deep pockets who buy a rural lot for more money than a 100-acre farm sold for a generation ago. The family farm is disappearing in favour of the factory farm. Our supermarket shelves are laden with genetically engineered Frankenfoods, and smog in rural areas can be just as bad as it is in the downtown core.

Against that backdrop steps the urbanite with a homesteading dream, a handful of seed catalogues and a composter. Such irrepressible optimism is healthy medicine for troubled times. It has certainly fuelled my adventure for the past two decades.

Urban and rural people can co-exist, despite the disparities in the cultures. Good fences, mutual respect and knowing whose woods you are stopping in are all helpful in making the transition. Sometimes the easiest thing to do is just relax and be yourself.

People do try. For instance, in an affluent, urban/rural community close to a big city, a same-sex wedding was planned for the child of longtime "weekend" residents who had inveigled themselves into the fabric of the community. It was a wedding that would see cattle ranchers and pork producers mingling with stock brokers and artists.

Not wanting to appear as rubes, members of the rural community were determined to celebrate the untraditional marriage exactly as they would the nuptials of any happy couple. City friends attending the wedding were terribly impressed by the level of sophistication they felt from the country guests. The flowers came from local gardens and the ceremony was performed next to a willow-lined pond on the wide expanse of the front lawn at the weekenders' farm. Everyone agreed the brides were beautiful.

Afterward, a wedding supper was served under large white tents adorned with twinkling lights. A special chef had been brought in and the menu was displayed at each place setting. Reading it, the farmers in the crowd found their necks stiffening almost involuntarily. One spoke for them all when he was heard to say, "Mother, what the heck sort of wedding is this? Nobody told me they were VEGETARIANS!"

The people of my own community provide me with terrific inspiration and material. They are always honest, both with me and about me. An urban and urbane writer I know took my suggestion and stopped for exceptional baked goods at the Village Bakery in Mount Forest when he was touring the southwestern Ontario countryside. Slyly, he asked the proprietors if I ever shopped there.

"She used to," said Doug, the co-proprietor, "but she's on a diet now." It is hard to have secrets in a small town.

There is a story in this volume about secrets and a very special one that my father kept for half a century. Now my parents are also learning that they can have no secrets, since they have retired to Mount Forest. I get full and complete reports on where they shop and what they are up to. Still, they did surprise me by showing up on a float in the Santa Claus parade. Things can happen in a small town that would never happen in the big city.

My companion of the heart and mind, Stephen Williams, also known as Moose, appears in all his glory in these pages. Although I spent many years farming by myself while Moose provided the fiscal fuel, I am pleased to report that he is growing in both his knowledge of agriculture and his affection for it. The constantly evolving partnership that we share is one of the pleasures of aging.

And it is hard to accumulate any wrinkle that is not a laugh-line when you are owned by a bull terrier. Wally the Wonder Dog continues to wag his way into the affection of everyone he meets. His clownish charisma is such that when we visit the Big Smoke and stay at the elegant, dog-friendly Metropolitan Hotel, the management sends Wally gourmet dog biscuits.

My publisher Kim McArthur remains effervescent and playful, despite the responsibility of having received an award as Entrepreneur of the Year. It is a privilege to be a member of her stable of writers.

Now and then I meet a person who says to me, "I'm moving to the country and I am going to do exactly what you've done." I smile and wish them well, but — considering some of the things I have done in my two decades on the farm — I find it quite frightening. Hopefully, I can help such dreamers and optimists to avoid some pitfalls, but I am afraid there is no easy way to wrestle sheep.

Marsha Boulton,

somewhere between Harriston and Mount Forest, Ontario, Canada

http://marshaboulton.tripod.ca

Letters from the Country
Country
IV

THE PUMP OUT

When I bought the farm a couple of decades ago, I was admittedly naive in presuming that country air was cleaner than city air and water that came from a well was potable. There were no industrial fumes emanating from the pastures and the water that ran from the tap was clear and cold. That the toilet flushed did not surprise me and there was scant discussion with the real estate agent about how it worked despite the lack of city services. Somewhere there was a septic system to manage such things. The exact location of the "head" of the septic system and the mysterious thing called a "weeping tile bed," did not concern me at the critical time of purchase when visions of wicker chairs on the renovated front porch took precedence.

But there comes the day when thoughts of floribunda rose gardens and outdoor decks disappear. That is the day when the plumber says the dread words: "Septic's backed up, you need to get it pumped out."

Then it hits you that all the time you have spent puttering around, dolling things up, applying gingerbread trim and affixing windowsill plant boxes has been a fantasy. Somewhere within a 20-second stroll from the front door there is an underground tank filled with the residue of what you have been flushing for years. And now you have gone and filled it up. It won't take another flush and you don't want to even think about using the plunger.

The first time this happened, spring was just beginning to permeate the winter frost. I was heartily confused about what to do until the plumber passed me the business card of a fellow he said could do the job.

I reached Mr. Marshall at home and he said he would be right over. He asked if we had cleared the tank head. I offered that I would try to find it.

The thing is that the septic system had never acted up before, so I had no idea where it began or ended. Years earlier, I planted a plum tree where I now understood my weeping tile bed was carefully laid out. I had wondered why all those red-clay tiles kept turning up in the soil when I dug the hole for the tree. Now I wondered how much of a weeping tile bed I had left and how much of it was tangled with the plum tree's bountiful root system.

Moose and I dug around a bit and finally his shovel struck metal. Carefully we removed the earth and discovered what looked like two rounded handles resembling scaled-down croquet hoops that were imbedded in concrete. Further earth removal revealed the concrete to be square-cut, and about half the size of a patio stone. It was a lid. Under normal circumstances, I would have assumed we had discovered some hidden treasure, but now I had a glimmer of septic system savvy.

We were standing carefully away from the discovery when Mr. Marshall's truck came roaring up the driveway.

I am told that in the old days such trucks were called "honey wagons," which gives you some idea of the sense of humour our forebears had. At any rate, there was certainly no hiding Mr. Marshall's truck from the neighbours. It was a storey-and-a-half black truck, draped with large hoses. The words "Marshall's Septic Cleaning" screamed out from the sides in lime-green letters.

The telephone rang before I had even greeted Mr. Marshall. It was my neighbour Ken "Hooter" Houston calling to say he'd seen Marshall's truck heading up the lane and he would be right over.

I had not considered the possibility that pumping my septic tank would become a public event, but it seemed inevitable. Next thing I knew, Hooter pulled up in his pickup with the brothers Sinclair in tow. They got out and greeted Mr. Marshall as though he was an old friend, pausing to jab Moose in the shoulder the way men do when they are gearing up for some big event.

When there are five men in the yard and only two shovels, a woman's work is done. The men took turns digging up various parts of the garden looking for more tank lids while I attempted to salvage crocus and daffodil bulbs from the piles of earth.

"Looks like it must be an old Sullivan tank," said Mr. Marshall, approvingly. "Darn fine tanks, double chamber and solid steel."

House-proud I might be, but septic-tank-proud I now felt. Without even knowing it, all these years I had been served by a "darn fine tank." I took some comfort in that.

The dirt kept flying as the men rotated between turns digging and turns sitting on the tailgate of Hooter's truck absorbing "fuel" from a case of 24. When the dust settled, three tank lids were cleared and the site looked like a movie set for a scene from trench warfare in World War I.

Mr. Marshall began uncoiling his hose. It was a corrugated sort of rubbery affair wide enough to roll a baseball through. Even though it was a very long hose, an extra piece had to be added to reach the tank lids. Mr. Marshall screwed the hoses together tightly, but it still made me nervous. A burst hose in range of my freshly washed kitchen windows loomed as a nightmare.

Moose helped Mr. Marshall remove one of the lids. I thought they were very brave. When they started tugging on the handles, I fled to an upstairs bedroom where I could observe the scene from a distance.

From my vantage, I watched as Mr. Marshall inserted the end of the hose deep into the ground. While the men leaned on shovels and sprawled around the picnic table, a motor in the truck roared to life. The hose shook and jiggled, but it stayed in the hole. Men straddled it, laughing and drinking beer. Then they sat down together and started swapping stories while the hose jiggled at their feet and the engine roared. None of them seemed remotely aware that something I consider deeply personal and private was working its way through the massive hose at their very feet and was being swallowed up into the truck in the lane.

This went on for an appallingly long time. In fact, it went on for precisely 53 minutes. I have no idea what the men were talking about, but everyone seemed to be having a heck of a good time.

When the roaring and jiggling finally stopped, Mr. Marshall calmly rewound his hoses and prepared to depart. He left the lane in a blaze of black and lime-green with Hooter and the Sinclairs following, waving and shouting something about a "darn fine pump out."

Wordlessly, Moose and I put the two shovels to work and levelled out the landscape, content to know that the Sullivan tank was ready to "receive" again, and somewhere a tile was weeping as it should.

THE DESIGNER FLOCK

All sorts of people choose to raise sheep. In my own limited experience I have met philosophers, truck drivers, poets, fashion models and coroners who raise sheep. In many ways, raising sheep has become the great Canadian hobby farm pastime. And one thing you can be sure of, if a new physician of the male persuasion is recruited to the service of a rural community, his wife will raise sheep. Not a lot of sheep; not enough sheep to make a living, but just enough sheep to keep the pastures mowed and barbeque sizzling. Wool and spinning may or may not be an issue, but there is usually an element of design to the flock.

My first country doctor's wife kept sheep. When that doctor moved on and the new one arrived, sure enough, his wife started raising sheep, too. Sometimes medical husbands are involved with the flock quite beyond the barbeque. Certainly they can supply useful drugs to keep their shepherd wives fit during lambing. More often, they are known to frustrate their spouses when asked a medical question by responding with the pronouncement, "How should I know? It's a sheep!"

The sheep who live with the wives of doctors are inevitably well-tended and pampered creatures of quality breeding. A new doctor's wife just has to consult the network of rural doctors' wives to get plugged into the appropriate sheep community and discover the names of the best breeders. They tend to acquire unusual breeds, since they are searching more for decoration than units of production. This adds a certain interest to their flocks since regular "trying-for-profit" shepherds seldom think of breeding colourful, compact Shetland sheep or wonderfully woolly Lincolns and Corriedales. It is always fun to see something different grazing in a pasture, even though it might not be practical.

So when my doctor's wife, Anne, called me one bright spring day to talk about sheep, I was expecting to hear that some lovely new bloodline was coming to the neighbourhood. Anne is a medical professional herself, a registered nurse, and a genuine character. The doctor in her life had been an army medico before settling in a small Ontario town, where they built a house on a small acreage of land overlooking a river. The property just happened to have a barn. The next thing she knew, Anne was acquiring sheep from other doctors' wives. Hers was always a flock of many names — Pumpkin, Mariella, Scooter, Esperanza, Flossie and all sorts of names that have been featured in Broadway musicals — Dolly, Maria, Eliza. There was even one husky-voiced ewe whom Anne named Eartha Bacall, because her *bah* had a purring hint of Eartha Kitt and the rough rasp of Lauren Bacall.

As it happened, Anne was not acquiring more sheep, she was dispersing them. Her children were grown. She had built her dream house. She had managed a bed and breakfast business and played almost every starring female role in every local musical production that had been mounted. Now, it was time for her to take her act on the road. Anne was embarking on an adventure as a nurse at a remote health care facility in the Great Canadian North. She was about to become a sort of bush pilot Florence Nightingale. I imagined her carrying her little black medical bag, wearing mukluks and white silk scarf and singing "The hills are alive . . ." as she tromped across the frozen tundra.

The question then became, "What to do with the sheep?" It seems Anne had been preparing for this adventure of hers for a couple of years and she had stopped keeping ewe lambs for breeding and had not added any new animals. Gradually, the named sheep were departing naturally to be buried in hillside plots that were marked by a sort of sheepish cenotaph surrounded by wild flowers.

At this point, Anne only had four ewes left, and all were past their prime. She did, however, have one middle-aged, black ram named Buckle who was a Canadian-bred Rideau Arcott. Anne said he was a fine lad who had produced some nice crops of lambs as well as some fine fleeces. She was offering to give me Bucky for free so that he would have a chance at a quality of life that included breeding, since she was planning to maintain her ewe flock as celibates. No one else had wanted the black ram and he was on the verge of being sent to market just as he reached his peak as a stud.

It could not have happened at a better time from my standpoint. I had relied on a father-and-son team of rams the previous season. Lord Randall, the senior ram, was an elegantly aging Suffolk ram. His son, Crash Test Dummy, was a carbon copy of old dad, with rough white wool and a solid black head that was hard as a rock and apparently filled with a substance of similar specific gravity. The problem was that young Dummy did not do particularly well in the breeding department. He had been given his allotment of ewes for a specific breeding period in a pasture well separated from his father and his father's harem. However, only half of those ewes produced lambs born within the framework of that breeding cycle. The others had lambs much later, probably sired by old — but — reliable Lord Randall.

Dummy was also an aggressive ram. I could not get into a pen with him without watching his every move or he would try to butt me. Once he was out in the field when my neighbour Ken "Hooter" Houston came over to assist me in farming. Ken was in the barnyard trying to figure out where the water pipe might have been run underground for some reason when I warned him to watch for the ram.

"I've got 35 years on the farm, don't you worry about me with a ram," laughed Hooter, without even looking up. "That darn ram tries anything and I'll . . ."

At that precise moment, the Crash Test Dummy ram crashed into Hooter's hind side, lifting him aloft. Hooter's legs shot straight out from under him. He looked like a startled cartoon character and the toque that he wore well into the month of May dangled from the side of his head.

Then the ram withdrew, suddenly. Hooter was poised in mid-air attempting to get out a good holler before he splatted to the ground, landing in a mess of spring mud and manure.

That was an unfortunate move on Dummy's part since Ken can usually be counted on as a reliable relief shepherd when I have to leave the farm for a day or two. Even the kindest and gentlest of good neighbours does not take kindly to being bruised and battered by a semi-impotent, woollen battering ram. Dummy was going to have to go. He sealed his own fate one day when he engaged his own father in battle and killed him. I found Dummy grazing peacefully beside poor Lord Randall who was quite plainly dead. Both of them had bloodied brows, and there was also blood on Randall's side where his son had apparently beaten him into the ground. People who think that sheep are gentle, timid creatures should have seen this terrible tableau of patricide.

Once I had rid the flock of Crash Test Dummy, I was ready to search for a new ram. Purebred sheep have always been my interest, but I was wearying of the paperwork and considering changing breeds. Anne's offer of a young black buck of a breed that has been growing in popularity appealed to me. So, too, did the designer possibilities.

Just as with horses, one should not look a gift ram in the mouth. I arrived at Anne's farm one lazy spring after-noon to pick up Bucky sight unseen.

When we arrived at the barn a collection of old ewes crowded at the gate, poking their grey muzzles at Anne and nudging her for a treat. They would spend the rest of their days on the farm, sharing a hay manger with the doctor's horses and leaning on each other for support. Bucky was cordoned off in a stall. It took a minute for my eyes to adjust to the dim light and when they finally did it took me another minute to control facial expression and ensure that I did not break out laughing.

I do not think that I've ever seen a sheep quite as funny looking as black Buckle. His head was short-cropped with a narrow muzzle that widened into a triangle, the far corners of which bore his small dark eyes. His ears flopped over much like a beagle's, while a long hunk of curled wool tossed between them in a cavalier manner. His body was short, squat and muscular. He moved with the deliberate pacing of an army cadet, although he was always slightly out of step, giving him a precarious state of motion. He was quite endearing, but hardly what one would think of as a "stud."

"You wouldn't think it to look at him," warned Anne, "but Bucky just loves his work. Sometimes I have trouble making him stop."

A better recommendation would be hard to find.

Anne was both sad and happy to see Bucky leave. He was sent off with a sack filled with apples, a blue halter and a special pair of pruning shears suited to lop off his tough toenails. The old lady ewes gathered at the gate to watch his departure. I do not know if their mournful *bahs* were those of regret or relief.

Bucky settled in at the farm straightaway. I put him in a pen with a view of the pastures and a private exercise yard under a shady apple tree where he could snooze or study the landscape. When Ken "Hooter" Houston saw the gentle, black ram, he asked me when I was going to get a real one.

"Looks to be a bit of a lightweight," said Ken, who admitted that he had no desire to tango with another hard-headed ram. "I mean any fellow that's going to have to handle 20 females at a time should have a bit more substance, don't you think?"

But when the time came, Bucky proved to be a true Lothario. He wore his harem-marking crayon with pride. After two weeks with a selection of ewes, all of them bore a yellow mark on their rump from the crayon harness that he wore around his chest. Bucky looked invigorated and his step seemed more sprightly than ever before. He bred the whole flock in several rotations, his crayon changing from yellow, to purple, to green and to red. Each marking signified a mating, from which I could predict the future lambing date of each ewe. Worn-out Bucky spent the late autumn snuffling through the grass for fallen apples.

That winter in the lambing shed was one of the most pleasant I have ever had. The big, white-bodied Suffolk ewes were round with lambs and when it came time to deliver them they seemed to spit the black lambs out like watermelon seeds. The lambs were small but they were vigorous. Some of them had long, curved Suffolk ears and others looked just like black Labrador retriever puppies. Their squat little bodies bore rippled black wool that was much softer than the wool of Suffolk lambs. And while the dark wool of Suffolk lambs is destined to turn white as the lamb grows, these lambs were destined to stay black, since dark-pigment DNA always wins over light. To me, that was the brilliant part.

By the end of May, the pastures had greened up and the earth was firm. I was ready to let the sheep out for a good romp. The ewes charged out of the barn full of fire, kicking up their heels in one direction while their udders flopped to the other side. The lambs froze in the doorway, uncertain and twitching with excitement. Then they bolted.

It was as close a moment as I am likely to get to being a doctor's wife. The white ewes buried their black Suffolk heads in the grass, grazing fiercely and gorging themselves. The black lambs flopped around them like rag puppets. The result was a study in perfect spring, done in black, white and green.

All summer the checkerboard flock entertained visitors. When I let out my long low whistle, they came running across the field — a player piano keyboard on hooves. That fall, I acquired a new Suffolk ram for my purebred ewes. He and Bucky became great pals. I kept some of the black ewe lambs because they were irresistible, and I allowed Bucky a few white girlfriends so that I could keep adding little black sheep to the barnyard. Every year, I will have some new shade of sheep; perhaps I will even begin casting about for a spinning wheel. I call it my "designer flock" — the ultimate in farm accessories.

WHY DOES THE TURTLE CROSS THE ROAD?

It happens every spring, just as soon as the peeper frogs begin chatting at the pond the turtles begin trying to cross the roads. And we turtle rescuers start helping them get to the other side.

I thought about that earlier this spring, when the ice was beginning to melt off the ponds and I drove past the swamp where I watch the turtles laze on a fallen log every summer.

Three new houses have been built near the swamp and tons of earth have been moved and removed along the narrow roadway. But the turtle log has been there for all the 20 years I can remember.

The roads that wind between swamps and ponds are curvy affairs lined with cedars and the occasional wild apple tree. These are less-than-travelled gravel-and-dirt roads where two cars going in opposite directions is "an event." Sometimes stretches of such roads remain untouched by the snowplow all winter long, but spring draws out the curious, who go for a weekend drive to check out the pond levels and see what damage winter might have wrought to certain favourite trees and vistas.

The turtle log is a big old hunk of wood, probably a fallen spruce tree, and it seats eight to ten, saucer-sized painted turtles quite nicely during the high season. The road bends and the sides dip off into long marsh grasses that edge a lily-pad-covered swamp spiked with the skeletons of decaying evergreens and tamaracks. Although it is close to the road, you have to know where to look to find the turtle log and once you find it, you don't tell anyone else about it because it is a special thing.

The trouble is that the little windy roads between swamps and ponds connect to bigger roads used by gravel trucks, milk trucks, school buses, tourists and local traffic. And that is a big problem for turtles that are looking for a place to bury their eggs.

The way it goes is that the turtles wake up in the pond after a long hibernation in the mud. Then they meet their fellow turtles and fall in love. I have never seen the courtship ritual of the painted turtles that live in the ponds near me, but I understand it has a special sort of romance to it.

The male, which is usually smaller than the female, swims backward and tries to get in front of the she-turtle. She takes a look and decides whether or not she likes the cut of his jib. If she does, she allows the male turtle to reach out to her and he vibrates his long front claws against her outstretched chin. Then she reaches back to embrace him and they sink to the bottom of the pond where mating occurs.

Not exactly muskrat love, but considering the fact that they are both wearing body armour, it must be a virtual engineering feat.

Then the female goes off to lay her eggs. Which brings her to the road.

Turtles like to lay their eggs in a warm sunny spot where the soil is loose enough for them to dig a hole. That sweet spot just beyond the soft shoulder of a roadway is perfect. She does her digging, lays anywhere from four to twenty white, leathery eggs, covers the nest and returns to her pond. Sometimes crossing the road in the process.

And so, you see it all the time these days. Squashed turtles in the road. I'm not suggesting that drivers should endanger their own lives or those of others to avoid tire contact with a turtle, but since turtles do tend to cross the road in daylight hours, we should at least be watchful.

Which brings me to the business of turtle road-rescue. This is something that must be done with care, for a variety of reasons.

First, when you spot a turtle in danger, one that is sitting spryly at the edge of a road facing the other side, or one that is already in transit, continue driving. Do Not Brake Suddenly For Turtles.

Find a safe place to turn around or pull over. Park your vehicle with flashers on and check for traffic. Approach turtle quietly but deliberately. The turtle will do one of two things: go into its shell and hope you go away or run away as fast as a turtle can run.

When you catch up to the turtle, scoop it up with both hands, holding the edge of the shell with your fingers at the widest part of the middle of the turtle where it has the least chance of kicking you away with its sharp claws or scaring you by turning its olive-coloured neck in biting mode. Do not mess with snapping turtles unless you have a snow shovel handy.

Move quickly to safety at the side of the road.

Now, stand still and hold the turtle away from your body and downwind of you, and anyone you have kind feelings towards, because that turtle is going to urinate for all its worth. Nothing personal, that is just the only defence mechanism a turtle has when it can't hole up in its shell or run away.

If you forget to do this the first time, you won't likely forget again.

Experienced turtle rescuers keep a cardboard box or a burlap sack in their vehicle for turtle management en route to their turtle log of choice. Otherwise, you end up with a turtle crawling all over your car, disappearing under floor mats and accidentally pressing those buttons that make car seats move forward and back and inflate or deflate lumbar regions.

Bicyclists who are transporting turtles should secure the turtle in a backpack, allowing sufficient aeration, but never enough space for the turtle to squirm through and get its claws around your ears.

Do not take the turtle home with you. Do not even think about it. Turtles are wild things. They will never learn to come or sit or stay. They can manage quite nicely without you, now that you have helped them get to the other side.

Do take the turtle to a nearby turtle log. Like me, you may have to watch your step and slide through a bit of bog before you get close enough to the water to let the turtle go. Once she sees the pond, she will run a few feet before diving in and sinking to the bottom.

If there are already turtles sunning themselves on the log, they will plop in the water.

Plop. Plop. Plop. It is a most satisfying sound.

Who knows, maybe they swim down to greet the new road-rescue.

And who knows, maybe all those turtles clinging to their logs every summer are the product of a turtle that some kind soul helped cross a road.

THE BIRDS EYE GARDEN

I envy those people who have the patience to plant a garden to a theme. For years I imagined myself having the courage to create a monochrome garden. Of course, the most precious of all would be a "white garden" in the tradition of British novelist and poet Vita Sackville-West. The idea of looking out on an all-white garden shimmering in the moonlight is an idle dream to me. Not that shimmering silver leaves and chalk pale petals would not be beautiful, but because I do not have the restraint required to control myself from stocking up on the whole palette of colour that leaps off the pages of seed catalogues as I patiently wile away the dark winter evenings.

The same is true of the vegetable garden. Why grow simple green beans when you can grown yard-long green beans and purple pod beans that turn green when you cook them? Variety is everything in a vegetable garden, along with little surprises and a touch of chaos. It is convenient to plant things in rows, but the rows don't have to run the same way.

I like a vegetable garden where I can be comfortable, so I want some fragrant nicotina and columbine there to greet me. And what could be more beautiful than a cascade of morning glories on the garden fence to watch while you are having breakfast and a lush row of four o'clock Marvel of Peru to open its blooms at tea time? A little organized confusion gives a garden some character.

However, gardening with a bull terrier gives confusion a whole new dimension. Wally seems to view every stage of gardening as something to be challenged.

When the Rototiller roared to life, it must have appeared to be an outdoor version of the snarling dragon, otherwise known as the vacuum cleaner. It took me two years of patience and perseverance to convince the dog that the vacuum is not some sort of soul-sucking device, with a hose in need of puncturing.

The Rototiller, with its churning tines and explosive gas engine, was more threatening, requiring Wally to bark at it constantly and loudly. After a few clods of dirt flew in his eyes, Wally got the notion to stand back while attempting to render the Rototiller silent. Good thing, too, because I did not want to have to bandage a mangled nose caught in the twisted steel that prepared the soil for planting.

There is something satisfying about looking over a cleared vegetable garden plot that has been worked with compost and manure and smoothed of clumps and bumps. All of that is disrupted when a bull terrier decides to turn it into a soccer playing field. Dirt flies, seams are gouged in the earth and when the dust settles, it settles on a dirty dog, who might just decide to have a serious roll in it for good measure.

Gardening should be a relaxing hobby. In my fantasy life, I wander through my garden wearing a long denim skirt, a flowing shirt and a straw bonnet. Like Mother Nature, my wicker basket brims with carrots and cauliflowers and radishes the size of a baby's fist. First, however, the garden must be planted. I have no fantasies about this. I bend over and shove the seeds in the ground one at a time, and I don't care much what I wear as long as it doesn't get in my way.

I was in just such a position, planting my third row of green peas, when Wally the Wonder Dog began to take an interest in gardening. The seeds were small, but they were round and rather ball-like. He dug his nose into the hoed row where I had carefully laid out the little green pea seeds. Then he flung his entire body across the row to prevent me from covering the sacred round objects. He lay there, wearing what looked like a self-satisfied grin.

Fine. I got down on my knees and proceeded to pat soil over the seeds until reaching the dog carcass, which I moved much as one would a wheelbarrow by hoisting the hind legs and turning. Undeterred, Wally decided that woman on a her knees needs a bull terrier around her shoulders.

This is pretty much the way the planting of the entire garden went. Sometimes whole packets of seeds were strewn accidentally when Wally burst through the garden with his soccer ball. I could see little green peas flying everywhere, and corn kernels and the occasional soft white zucchini seed. Any seed smaller than a green bean could have drifted anywhere. A plastic mesh fence around the garden was ineffective as anything except a hurdle. Wally "watered" the poles I had pounded in to mark the rows.

The resulting garden was a kind of marvel that varied from disaster to brilliance. You could find a tossed salad in just about every row — radish here, cucumber there, here a romaine there an endive — that sort of thing. A whole row of snow peas flourished, with a couple of huge sunflowers dropped in for good measure. Squash and pumpkin vines wound their way around corn stalks. In some sections of the garden I transplanted nursery-bought egg plants, broccoli and Brussels sprouts. They looked quite organized until carrot and beet seeds began sprouting all around them. My friend Naomi called it "Birds Eye" — after the company that first marketed frozen mixed vegetables.

If the method of its planting made the garden slightly inaccessible, it also made it unconventionally easy to tend. I could not rototill between the rows because the rows were no longer clear. So I laid down barn boards to make walkways, and piled old straw and grass clippings around plants that were in areas that were difficult to navigate. Sweet peas and scarlet runner beans grew up, over and around a blue wooden chair with a cracked seat that seemed to suit the garden. Although it appeared to have no rhyme or reason, in its absolute randomness there was character and sensibility.

When harvesting the bounty, I used a sort of search-and-pluck method. The result were many satisfying tin-foil-wrapped packets of barbequed vegetables at dinner-time. One baby squash, a handful of green beans, slices of onion, a perfect cob of corn and a sweet red pepper, all chopped into manageable pieces, spritzed with olive oil, drizzled with balsamic vinegar and romanced with fragrant herbs make a wonderful side dish to grilled lamb chops.

I think one year of total chaos in the vegetable patch is about all I can manage. To preoccupy Wally, a new soccer playing field has been created beside the garden, so that we can keep an eye on each other while maintaining a healthy distance. He knows that I will not begrudge him the occasional foray into the garden, and I have found him rather useful at digging up potatoes. I have kept some of the planks to use as walkways through the garden in places where I do not want straight and narrow rows, and I definitely intend to throw some sunflower seeds around just to see where they sprout.

As a thanks to Wally for helping me learn to loosen up in the vegetable patch, I am planting some supersweet Tom Thumb tomatoes that he can eat straight off the vine.

Vita Sackville-West would never approve of my less-than-subtle gardens, but in many ways we are quite alike because we both adore arranging things in dirt. Vita once wrote that: "The man who has planted a garden feels that he has done something for the good of the world." I imagine Wally felt that way, too.

THE MYOTONIC GOATHERD

When I agreed to take the Myotonic Goat, I had no idea that it would turn into a kind of Heritage Moment filled with surprises. In fact, the goat was that least expected of things that gladdens the heart.

Since one of my off-farm jobs is promoting my books and speechifying, I am always meeting people. Some of them stay in touch with me and some of them appear out of the blue when I least expect them. Carol's e-mail about the goat certainly seemed to come from nowhere. I had met her five years earlier and we had chatted about her plans to move to the country and raise goats. Goats never having been my creature of choice, I politely offered that were I ever to have a goat I thought I would want one of those kinds that faint. I had seen pictures of such goats, and they seemed to be most unusual. Also, the idea that someone would feed and care for an animal every day of its life just so they could say "Boo" and watch the animal fall to the ground struck me as more than odd.

24

Five years later, Carol remembered our conversation and she e-mailed to offer me exactly one such goat, because, in fact, she is not the sort of person who wants to keep feeding and caring for an animal whose only likely use is as a party trick. True to her game plan, Carol now raises large, meaty white Boer goats with her husband, Gene, and makes a respectable supplemental income at it. A western breeder who supplied Carol's breeding stock had slipped in a goat of a different sort, perhaps as an amusement, but when feed prices start to climb and human resources are stretched just to care for the animals that are working for a living, even the most amusing of animals becomes a burden. Of course, I agreed to take the goat. With so many useless and retired mouths to feed already, I figured that it might be nice to lose money by feeding something completely different.

I had just begun to investigate the wonderful world of goats that drop like flies when Carol wrote again to advise me that the goat appeared to be pregnant. This was a great relief to me, since I already knew that goats enjoy the companionship of other goats. Now my clever new goat was off making her own friend. Carol thought the blessed event would occur about the same time as my sheep began to have their spring lambs. Terrific!

I had not seen any farms in the neighbourhood advertising myotonic goats for sale. In fact, I had rarely seen a herd of goats of any type. Any people I knew who had goats kept them largely for fun, for browsing rough brush areas and for their milk, which often ends up as cheese or yogurt. I had heard a story about buying a fainting goat at an auction, but when the new owners got it home the goat would not faint and they were disappointed. They must have felt quite stupid, standing around clapping their hands, honking horns and generally trying to figure out ways to scare a goat that just stood and looked at them.

I soon discovered that myotonics are a relatively rare type of goat. They have been called everything from "epileptic" to "nervous," to "stiff-legged" and "wooden-legged," but most commonly they are called "fainters." All of which is quite a misnomer, since they do not actually faint. Sometimes, when they are startled or excited, their muscles "lock up" and stiffen, causing them to lose their balance and fall over. It has to do with defects in the chloride channels in the muscle membrane that cause interference with the transmission of electric impulses within the muscle. Next thing you know the goat falls over. They are not in pain and they are fully conscious throughout, recovering quickly and carrying on doing goatish things. Some myotonic goats are more myotonic than others. For instance, some myotonics are so excited by the sound of grain in a feed bucket that they fall over in front of the feed trough, while others can find themselves in a confrontational position with a belligerent donkey and still manage to keep their footing.

Myotonic goats are considered to be a native American breed, but the truth is they came from Canada. The story is something of an agricultural legend. As it goes, around about 1880 a man named John Tinsley showed up on the doorstep of Mr. J.M. Porter in Marshall Country, Tennessee. Tinsley was travelling with a cow, which he called a "sacred cow" so it may have been an Indian

Zebu, a lanky beast with floppy ears and a hump at the shoulder. Three doe goats and a buck rounded out the travelling menagerie. The whole lot of them had come to the middle of Tennessee from Nova Scotia and Tinsley spoke in a thick brogue. Americans described the Eastern Canadian's headgear as being "fez-like"; however, they may have never seen a toque at that time. His clothing was also "unusual" and everything about the stranger was a bit odd, including his goats, which seemed to have periodic fainting spells, the likes of which no one had ever seen.

John Tinsley was working on the Porter Farm when a local animal lover, Dr. H.H. Mayberry, visited and observed the goats. He offered John Tinsley the princely sum of $36 for the four animals but Tinsley refused, only to show up later that year with the goats in tow and his wallet open. Subsequently, Tinsley worked for Dr. Mayberry, and his quirky reputation grew as he refused to eat meals at the dinner table, preferring the company of his cow. After three weeks of this, Tinsley departed with his sacred cow, ending up at Lick Creek, Tennessee, where he met an older woman named Bramhill. They married and he farmed her land through one crop. Then Tinsley hit the road with his cow again and nothing more was ever heard from him.

Dr. Mayberry started breeding the goats and gradually they spread throughout the countryside, sometimes mingling with other breeds of goat. By the middle of the twentieth century, the myotonic goat population had dwindled. Sometimes farmers culled stiff-legged goats, thinking there was something wrong with them. Fainting goats were also said to have been used by shepherds, who made them literal scapegoats. They would add a few myotonics to a large sheep flock so that if wolves decided to run down their dinner, all they would take was a myotonic that had fallen over out of fear. Such was the life of a rare goat that could not stay on its feet.

By the late 1980s, myotonics were becoming endangered, and fanciers roamed the countryside searching for survivors. Some of these goats were crossed with other breeds, creating small ones and colourful ones for the exotic pet market. Lately, myotonics have been crossed with big meaty Boer goats in hopes that the muscling of the myotonic would mix with the size of the Boer to produce a tender meaty goat. Collectively, the goats called "myotonics" share the unique genetic characteristic of stiffening muscles, an ungoatly aversion to jumping over fences, a certain bulging to their eyes and endearing ears that poke sideways. They come in all sorts of colours and sizes.

I did not ask what colour goat Carol and Gene were bringing to me. When "Mya the Myotonic" arrived one brisk Saturday morning in February, I was delighted to find her to be a goat of many colours — brown, tan, white, black, even grey. Her horns curl backward gracefully like her short black goatee and her stunted tail pokes upward like a docked dog's, twitching. Mya has lovely amber eyes, a soft black muzzle and a definite goat smell. Gene carried her from his truck to the waiting pen, so I figure she weighs less than a sack of grain. Taller than Wally the Wonder Dog, she is nowhere near as stocky or thickly muscular and much more deer-like.

Carol gave me a quick course in goat herding, which is very much like sheep herding, with some variations.

Mya was isolated to allow me to get used to her ways and watch her so that I would know what her "normal" behaviour was. Also, she was so much smaller than the full-fleeced pregnant ewes that I feared she would be crunched trying to get to the grain trough, if she didn't faint. We could look at her in her pen from the family room in the house, and it was interesting to watch her exploring and adapting to her new home.

Just before she left, Carol and I talked about the upcoming "kidding." The new goat would have a Boer father and it would not be myotonic. The gene skips one generation. So if the baby was a female and she was bred back to a myotonic goat her offspring would stiffen. This was Mya's first kidding but no problems were anticipated. Carol warned me that iodine on the newborn's navel would likely not be necessary since goats tend to nip them off quite short naturally. We had covered all bases and I would have plenty of time to read up on all aspects of goats while waiting for my herd to grow.

Wrong. The very next day — the historic day on which Canada's Men's Olympic Hockey Team matched the effort of the Women's Olympic Hockey Team by winning Gold — Moose paused to look out the window at the goat and noticed some movement around her. The pen she was in had been the pheasant hunting ground of the fowl-killing mink and he feared the worst. We ran out to the pen just before the Canadian team scored their go-ahead goal and we found a baby goat.

Tiny, she was. A tiny creature done in shades of beige with black streaks down her legs and a grey topline stripe that stopped in a sworl on her forehead. She looked like a furry stuffed toy. Sweet of face and fleet of hoof, the doe-ling was on its feet and nursing as though being born was an everyday thing. Mya was quiet and performing perfectly. Proving the old adage that a goat will eat anything, she quietly chewed the afterbirth.

I was glad the kidding had occurred in a confined space, since I had heard that myotonics sometimes liked to hide their young like wild deer. In the pen, I could touch the baby, and Mya did not seem to mind a bit. Wally the Wonder Dog poked his big nose through the pen door and whined. He stepped forward cautiously, tail beating so fast there was a breeze. Mya allowed him to approach just to a certain point before lowering her horns almost imperceptibly. Wally got the message and he booted it out of the pen.

I sent pictures to Carol, who was surprised the birth had occurred in such a short time. When she saw the doeling it was obvious to her that Mya had not been bred by an over-sized, stolid Boer goat. Instead Carol attributed the deed to "Dirty Larry," a lively pygmy goat that was a favourite pet of her grown daughter, Emily. Carol advised me that this little goat was bound to be a "hoot." We named her Toni, so the spring-made sign on their pen and pasture will read "Mya and Toni, the Myotonic Goats."

I am enjoying my instant goat herd. Pygmy goats are excellent jumpers and Toni races around her pen jumping up and over a bale of straw with fleet ease. Mya pays less and less attention to Wally giving the baby doe a sniff. I can only hope that Toni will learn how to butt soccer balls so that they can play happily ever after.

As a rule, I am finding goat chores take a lot less time than the time spent petting goats. They seem to prefer eating grain out of my hand. One word of warning, however. Never listen to the soundtrack of *The Sound of Music* if you have a goat or you will be forced to hear the regrettable Rogers and Hammerstein song "The Lonely Goatherd" endlessly in your mind and the words "Lay ee odl lay ee odl lay hee hoo" will start to make sense to you.

I have yet to see Mya the Myotonic goat faint. She has never so much as bristled, let alone stiffened. Like her non-fainting miniature daughter, she has huge curiosity about the world around her and she shows no sign of fear. I don't want watching my goat falling down to become a public spectacle. I don't want lovely young Toni to be tripping over her mother because something unexpected occurs to trigger a genetic oddity. In fact, I would be perfectly happy if my fainting goat never has cause to faint.

THE DINKY SHEEP

Dinky was a funny kind of sheep. Short and squat, she had the full body of a regular Suffolk sheep, but she seemed to have been cut off at the knees, rather like a dachshund. Carrying the lowest head in the flock did not bother her and she used her stature — or lack of it — to her advantage when she pushed her way to the feed trough.

I bought Dinky as part of a package of ewes from a woman who was leaving the business. Dinky was neither young nor old for a ewe. I was told that her lambs were normal-sized and grew up to have fine long legs. She had always had twin lambs and all of them were female. If that was not enough to recommend the little ewe, she also had an expressive face and a way of tilting her head towards you when you spoke. Some sheep breeders would have been ashamed to have a stunted creature in their flock, but I rather liked the look of her and she came at a discount price.

I had four sets of fine twin ewe lambs from Dinky. She was a good mother and never needed assistance. Her lambs grew tall and straight, and if they were lucky they inherited their dam's expressive face. Sheep like Dinky are a shepherd's delight.

One year, Dinky was the last ewe in the flock left to lamb. She was getting up in years but the pregnancy seemed to have gone well. Her woolly body swelled and she mumbled sheep curse words when she had trouble getting to a standing position. Every morning when I visited the barn I expected to see twin lambs happily suckling at her side.

About this time, to my surprise and delight, I was asked to take a freelance editing job for a few days a week in the Big Smoke. These bonus jobs and bonus paycheques often translate into farm improvements or new livestock and they are not to be treated lightly. I had to start right away, leaving the expectant Dinky in the care of Moose.

There are things to do with sheep that Moose has never shown any interest in. Midwife chores are among them. He likes to observe the lambs streaking around the barn and bouncing in the field, but sheep obstetrics just does not interest him. After some cajoling, I convinced him that Dinky was a do-it-herself kind of ewe. The only thing he would have to do was to daub the navels of her lambs with iodine. Dinky would do the rest.

Before I left for the city, I set up a receiving pen, fluffed with straw and ready to greet a new lamb family. There was a lot of stress involved in leaving the barn full of babies, but they did not seem to care that I was departing. The ewes barely looked up from their hay feeders. Dinky just gazed intelligently in my direction and heaved a long sigh.

At work the next day, I was embroiled in the delicate task of straightening out contorted sentences that had something vaguely to do with women's fashion. The phone rang just after lunch.

"She did it," said Moose. "I didn't even see it, they were just there after I did the morning chores. They are huge. Really huge lambs. Two of them. Both black. And they have tails."

He was talking faster than an auctioneer on methedrine. After congratulating him on a terrific job, I asked a few pertinent questions and sent Moose back to the barn to put iodine on the new arrivals' navels.

Half an hour later he was back on the line.

"I did it," Moose announced joyfully. "Didn't know how much iodine to use. So I filled a margarine tub up with the stuff and put the wet dangly bit in it all the way up to the belly. Spilled some. Sure stinks. Oh yeah, I think they're girl lambs. But they are so big you would think they were boys."

I could almost smell the iodine over the telephone. I asked if they were finding mother's milk and had round bellies.

"Oh yes, they're eating all the time," said Moose. "Dinky just *bahs* at them and they belly right up to the bar. I got my head right down there to make sure they were sucking and boy, oh boy, they are really drinking a lot of that milk. Gotta go, they might need burping now. And Dinky should get some warm molasses water, right?"

And so it went the whole afternoon. Moose with his head in the iodine-soaked straw watching the new lambs.

Moose mixing up molasses water to feed to Dinky so that her milk would flow. You would think that nothing had ever been born on the farm. When I finally bade Moose good night from my hotel room, he was tired, but insisted that he would take one more round of the barn just to be sure that "the girls" were doing well.

The next day was quieter. I had two phone calls at work that were not from Moose, which I took as a sign of a certain professionalism on both our parts. Moose now had a "Dinky Lamb" sheet in the barn on which he recorded various facts and observations about the new lambs. The largest of the two had the thickest tail and little wrinkles around her nose. The smaller had a sworl of black hair on her forehead that turned clockwise. They slept together in a clump but when they were awake they hopped and jumped and bumped heads with each other. Their tails wagged when they drank milk, and they drank a lot of milk. All the other animals were just fine, but Moose was spending "quality time" watching Dinky's lambs grow. Oh yes, the lambs had names — Smidget and Gidget — and they were truly exceptional.

After three days in the city, I was anxious to return to the farm to see these lambs that apparently had genius IQs, Hollywood star potential and the ability to secure world peace. I was packing the last of my things for the trip home when the phone rang.

"I didn't do it," sobbed Moose. "I didn't do a thing."

It took a little while to get him calmed down. It seems he had gone out to do the evening chores. Tossed the grain in the troughs and set out the hay for the main flock. Then he got Dinky her special grain dish and went to set it in the pen for her. She looked up at Moose, turned her head to the side as she always did with such grace. Then her legs buckled under her and she died.

Well, there was no consoling Moose. The plain fact was that Dinky was an old sheep. She had put all of her energy into giving birth to her lambs and she just checked out naturally with her babies at her side. There was nothing I could have done to prevent her departure and nothing Moose could have done.

Those few hours between Dinky's death and my return to the farm were fitful for Moose. I gave him instructions on mixing the "Lamb-Mo" brand lamb milk replacer powder that I keep on hand for orphan lambs. It is thick, gooey stuff that makes quite a mess out of the blender, and putting the plastic lamb nipples on the bottles can be a trying affair. Of course, he was concerned that the lambs would be terribly upset, so he removed them to the house where he tried to keep them quiet in a laundry basket lined with new towels that he had given me for Christmas. By the time I arrived home the kitchen was a chaos of bawling lambs, sticky countertops and the distinct odour of barnyard. Moose was sitting in a wicker chair in the middle of it all, holding a half-filled bottle of Lamb-Mo and looking like a widower after a war.

The lambs stayed in the house that night. Moose did not want them to return to the scene of the traumatic event until Dinky was removed and buried. Once their bellies were full of warm milk, they snuggled right into a little box that was placed within the warmth of the wood stove. Moose was right. They were darn fine lambs. After several cycles through the washing machine, my towels were fully recovered. It took Moose a few days to get back up to speed.

Smidget and Gidget became Moose's hobby. He helped prepare their lamb bottles and monitored their progress. Bottle-fed lambs seldom grow as quickly as well as their more fortunate contemporaries, but these two ewe lambs thrived. Like all of Dinky's previous lambs, their legs grew long and straight.

There was no parting with the two lambs, even though a good shepherd would not keep bottle babies as breeding stock. They have not been raised to observe motherly sheep behaviour, so they are sometimes poor mothers themselves. Since as babies they learned to be totally reliant on a human for food and behavioural response, they are generally giant pests as adults. Moose knew my feelings about this, so he made quite sure that "his girls" behaved themselves. When visitors came and we took them on walks through the woods, the Dinky daughters always followed along behind Moose. Of course, I could not send them off to the market. Smidget and Gidget lived long lives on the farm, and always had twin lambs of their own.

I never left Moose alone with expectant sheep again. Not all of them could be trusted to be as considerate as Dinky, waiting to die until she saw her lambs were in good hands. She was definitely a good sheep that came in a small package.

BULLY GOATS GRUFF

Goats can be the clowns of the barnyard, provided they stay in the barnyard. Goats outside of the barnyard become huge pests and inventive destroyers of just about everything. Goats seem to think it is a sort of "hurrah for you" sign when a human puts her hands on her waist and turns red in the face while saying short words very quickly.

I could not put Mya the Myotonic Goat in the pen with the sheep and lambs because the sheep hated the goat. This does not mean all sheep hate all goats all the time. The sheep would have hated a cow or a donkey equally. When their lambs are young they simply do not want to share space with anything that does not smell and look like a sheep. They express themselves by head-butting the intruder and they are rough.

Mya took her bashing like a goat and ran away before any damage was done. In the meantime, her two-week-old doeling, Toni, hid out with the lambs in the "creep," the private, rumpus-room style pen where lambs can play and eat and butt heads away from their mothers. The lambs sniffed the tiny goat and nibbled her little ears. That was too much for Toni who fled from the pen and ran off to be with her mother.

The goats were fine living together in a spacious pen. I added bales of straw for them to leap on and hide behind. Toni tried to climb a pole that supported a bird perch in the pen. They had shelter from the wind and snow and a picture window onto the laneway, so they could watch all the comings and goings. When Wally the Wonder Dog played soccer in the lane, the baby goat stood at the front of the pen watching him while he showed off.

After a week or so, Moose got the notion that goats should be free. Don't ask me where these notions come from. In the morning, when he checked his chickens, he opened the goat pen and Mya and Toni hopped out. By the time I went out to do the chores, the two goats had run rings around Moose and they were positively giddy. There were still snowdrifts covering the garden and the flower beds, so the goats were limited in the damage they could inflict.

Young Mya seemed to forget she was a new mother and took to jumping in the air and waving her horny head around. Little Toni was like a Furby on methedrine. *Zip, zip, zip*, the little beige goat climbed bales of hay until she was poking her head on the roof. She climbed the wood pile and she tottered along the top of a rail fence like a ballerina on barbed wire. Much faster than her mother, the breadbox-sized doeling could run full tilt around the chicken pens and end it all by leaping on an upturned hay feeder and stopping dead in her tracks.

Wally watched the goats with some surprise. The athletic moves they performed were as close to a full-blown bull terrier "hucklebutt" as Wally had ever seen. For those who have never seen a hucklebutt, it is a random act of frenetic activity in which the dog attempts to defy the laws of physics and gravity, with careless disregard for anything that gets in his way. Soon Wally was putting on his own display, flying around the yard, up and over the picnic table, around the cedar tree, across the front porch, heading directly for the wood pile and veering off into the haystack for a soft landing.

Perhaps the goats viewed this outburst as a challenge. They took off at full bore, heading down the lane towards the front of the house. Mya's udder was swinging as she threw her body around, twisting in the air and landing on all fours. Toni was galloping so fast her feet just skimmed the ground. Wally lay at my feet, flat on his belly with all legs splayed while he wagged his tail and made encouraging dog sounds. *Aroo, aroo.*

They came to blows that afternoon. I was in the house, where I could catch glimpses of the goats running circles around the house through the kitchen window. Moose insisted on making it a one-day experiment and I must admit it was amusing. Wally kept chasing his soccer ball around and nosing his smaller balls at the goats in an attempt to interest them. Only Toni would follow the roll of the ball but chasing it seemed to take far too much focus for a baby goat with a new world to explore.

They were all on the front porch together when Wally let out a dog holler. It was a yelp of pain and surprise. I found goats and dog at opposite ends of the porch

— frozen. Then Wally made a mad dash for the kitchen and the goats disappeared like deer after the first shot of hunting season is fired.

Wally quivered and cowered and curled up on his bed with his head tucked under his tail. Moose called him out and ran his hands over every inch of Wally's muscular body. There was no visible damage, no wincing and no limping. However, Wally was not about to revisit the outdoors. He heard the braying of the goats and whimpered.

The goats were returned to their pen. Their faces remained innocent, but something had gone on between them and the dog. I suspect it was something to do with horns and head butts.

Some people think that bull terriers are tough dogs, and they are in many ways. Wally once walked off the edge of a cliff in a gravel pit and he slid a good three stories to the ground. We ran down a path frantically, expecting to find him unconscious at best. Instead, he had left the scene of his landing and was off taking a swim in the quarry pond as though nothing had happened.

In the same vein, some people think goats are harmless creatures, and they are as long as anything you do not want to have harmed is kept away from them. I have been warned that goats have a peculiar appetite for the vinyl trim on cars. Apparently, they also like to jump on cars. They have been known to go through a car's sunroof, either because the sunroof was open or because the goat was too heavy for the sunroof. Once a goat is inside a car, they like to nibble on everything from the upholstery to the insurance papers.

Everything has its place in a barnyard and the goats will have to learn to stick to theirs and like it. They sealed their fate when they bullied Wally, even "free-goat" Moose agreed they had gotten too rough. The goats will still be able to watch Wally playing soccer from their pen, and maybe one at a time I will try gradually reacquainting them on neutral territory.

Once the pastures are ready, the sheep and the goats and the horses will have a huge space to carve into their own domains. Wally will be able to thread his way through them to inspect his groundhog holes, safe in the knowledge that he is the farm porch clown. And the clown goats will have green acres in which to play out their crazed antics.

BABE MOMENTS — GOLDEN AND TRUE

There is a scene in the 1995 movie *Babe* that expresses a moment that is instantly recognizable to anyone who has ever cared for a sick animal. It occurs towards the end of the movie when the audience is fully aware of the circumstances of the piglet Babe, his talking farm animal friends and his special bond with the farmer, Arthur Hoggett.

The pig is refusing to eat and the veterinarian tells Farmer Hoggett that the future looks bleak unless the pig at least drinks something. The farmer has already brought Babe into the house to warm him up and they sit together on the rumpled kitchen sofa that is a fixture in so many farm households. Tenderly, Farmer Hoggett takes the pig's weary head and places it on his lap, holding a baby bottle full of fluid and trying to poke it between the pig's lips.

"Come on, pig, come on, there's a good boy," says Farmer Hoggett, gently scratching the pig between its ears, where pigs do so love to be scratched.

Then the farmer looks down at the feeble animal and begins to sing to it in a soft voice. The notes were originally composed by Camille Saint-Saens for his organ *Symphony No. 3 in C-minor*, and the film score lyrics by John Hodge are a kind of a lullaby:

> *If I had the words to make a day for you,*
> *I'd sing you a morning golden and true.*

The pig begins to suckle and Farmer Hoggett's singing becomes more inspired, lifting him to his feet where he begins to step-dance around the room. There is joy in his face and his feet, and the pig recovers to win the sheep-pig day.

One critic I read suggested that the scene was intended to illustrate that the farmer was as daft as the pig. That critic had never tended a sick animal. The extremes one will go to in healing an animal are as heartfelt as those of a parent to a child. A little song and dance to a piglet is just the tip of the iceberg.

I have most certainly sung songs to animals, in sickness and in health. In fact, I have a whole tape of Frank Sinatra singing sheep songs that I like to play during lambing. Songs like "Ewe Make Me Feel So Young," "Ewe and the Night and the Music" and "I've Got Ewe Under My Skin" are old sheep standards to me. Sheep don't care how loud you sing or how off-key you get, and they can't dance worth a darn.

Like parents who stay up all night with feverish, restless babies, farmers will sit with a sick animal waiting for a breakthrough, offering water, special treats and words of comfort. In the case of shepherds, there is a tradition of bringing chilled lambs into the farm kitchen to warm them up in a box beside the wood stove. It is the kind of tradition that is recalled fondly in memory; however, when it actually happens, the stress of it can be enormous and the practicality is questionable.

I have found that the lamb that is warmed by the fire is invariably a weak triplet or the runt miracle of a set of quadruplets. It is usually discovered in the middle of the night during a blizzard, and ferrying it from the barn to the house involves wading through waist-high snowdrifts. Once the lamb is in the house, it does not leave before morning.

If the lamb is badly chilled or crusted in frost, it may be necessary to "thaw" it gradually, by placing it in a bucket of warm water and gently cradling its head. A lamb that needs this treatment will not protest until it is revived, but if the lamb does not need this treatment, it will kick and struggle and squirm and the bucket of warm water is bound to topple.

The lamb must be fed, preferably with colostrum, the first milk taken from an ewe that has just had her lambs. I always try to keep a small supply frozen for just such occasions. Once the lamb has its fill and is settled in its towel-lined box beside the fire, the logical thing would be to go to bed. But it does not work that way, because lambs do not sleep through the night anymore than babies do. Humans have to keep taking a look and giving a pat to the lamb. Even family dogs and cats take an interest. The next thing you know the teapot is on and someone is singing the lamb a song.

I have learned to do my best to keep farm animals in the barn, although I know of people who have stabled everything from orphan calves to foals and llamas in mud-room areas just outside their actual houses. Not only do such heart-wrenching interventions often turn out tragically, but they also entirely negate the purpose of a mud room.

Even keeping semi-domesticated animals such as ferrets in a house can cause havoc. A friend's young daughter had two ferrets of opposite sexes who managed to escape from their cages one night and promptly fell in love. Their sexual escapades became a feast that moved from one room to another for several days, during which time the ferrets screamed and moaned in carnal abandon, all the while staying one step ahead of capture.

More often than not, animal behaviour should occur in the environment of the animals. Even orphan lambs will do better if they are allowed to integrate with other lambs when they are not having their bottle feedings. There is something profoundly special and magical about sitting in a barn on a bale of straw in the middle of the night while all the other animals sleep and the lamb sucks on its bottle, waiting at the end to be burped and put back into its pen.

There are also far less gentle moments that occur as a part of animal husbandry. Calves that are too large are sometimes pulled from the womb using chains and leverage. The sharp milk teeth of piglets are clipped almost as soon as they are born, and castration, no matter how it is done, is still castration. The sights a farmer sees often scar the memory. The day the veterinarian removed the horns from a pair of my Highland cattle steers was as gruesome as I ever want to recall, since blood streamed and spurted from the clipped horns.

I have often felt that veterinarians invite farmers to share in the healing process so that we will learn respect for their craft. We bring the warm water and we hold the heads while their rubber-gloved hands go places we have never been. Vets have seen many things and it is hard to surprise them, but there are always little tricks they can teach.

I had a bloated ram in dire straits. He had eaten too much lush pasture and one or more of his four ruminant stomachs had swelled to the point of almost bursting. I had the ram haltered and tied outside in the pasture when the vet arrived. Without time to waste, the vet took out a trochar — a plastic implement about four inches long, which was twisted like a corkscrew with a flat lid and a hole at one end. The vet felt down the left side of the ram and told me to hold him steady. Then he rammed the trochar into the side of the ram's gut. I felt as though time stopped.

The vet then moved to quickly grasp the ram's head and he told me to stand at the ram's side and gently, but firmly, nudge and press up on his belly with my knee. I started to do this and without any warning a great huge wad of green grass and bile goop squirted forcefully out of the swollen ram all over my upper body. All I remember thinking is, "Interesting, this is very warm and green." I had certainly learned a lesson.

Had the pressure of stomach bloat not been relieved, the ram would have died. As it was, the ram ended up oozing green bile from the trochar site for about a week. The animal did not even seem to notice. I discovered that there is no Hint From Heloise that will help to remove the green stain of frothy bloat from a white T-shirt.

Keeping animals alive can become surreal. Early in my career as a lamb midwife, I encountered all sorts of problems that I now consider routine. If a lamb did not appear with the nose and two front legs coming first, I considered it a crisis situation. The first place I ran to was my library and one specific volume, *The TV Vet Sheep Book,* a British publication that is 30 years old. There, in Chapter 39 on "Malpresentations" I could find the solution in one of 47 graphic photographs. How many times that book has joined me on a bale of straw at midnight in the barn, I could not tell you.

I still look at what the TV Vet has to offer just before lambing begins to remind myself of what to do when a lamb decides to enter the world backwards or two lambs are tangled. Once learned, the trick of rotating a lamb that is coming backwards and getting it out quickly is not to be forgotten. Two lambs in the birth channel takes time, patience and sometimes a few strands of butcher twine to slip loosely around the closest head and legs, just to keep track of which lamb is coming first. Small hands are great assets.

Lambs that have to struggle to get into the world are often weak upon arrival. Usually, once their nostrils and throat are cleared, they will sputter to life. Other times, they can appear dead, although the heart is still beating, and these are the lambs that often become candidates for fireside boxes.

However, the TV Vet has another plan, which involves swinging the proverbial cat. You take the newborn lamb and grasp both back legs above the hock. You hold them securely in your strongest hand. Then you haul back and literally swing the lamb around a few times — over your head, arms straight out.

Just like the picture in the TV Vet book on page 131 of the Fifth Edition, I swing my lambs outdoors where I can be sure there are no walls or beams on which to bean them. The TV Vet does not wear a shirt in the photograph, but I have had excellent results fully clad.

Many lambs discover that life is worth living after a few swings around under a starry sky. Returned to their mothers, they seem to have a purpose and head forcefully for the udder and the beginning of their careers as habitual eaters.

Those moments are worth a song, when an animal takes the help that a human offers and then goes back to being an animal without questioning why. It is a unique kind of interspecies trust.

The narrator in the film *Babe* calls the pig "an unprejudiced heart," and such is true of all animals. So when a human can help them along the way, it is bound to make a day seem "golden and true." In fact, it is such a gift that the ending of Farmer Hoggett's song expresses the perfect wish:

> *I would make this day last for all time,*
> *Then fill the night deep in moonshine.*

SHEILA'S MOUSE

Sheila's dog found the mouse nest before she did. It was hidden in the back corner of a pantry at the lakeside cottage where mice, squirrels and the occasional skunk traditionally took cover for the winter. Three generations of Sheila's family had battled the varmints into retreat every spring. Then they spent the remainder of the summer luring chipmunks to the front veranda with peanuts.

Gabby, Sheila's chubby beagle, was probably just defending his kibble, which Sheila kept in a tightly lidded, metal garbage pail. After years of experience, she had learned that anything in the pantry that was not protected by steel was vulnerable to tiny gnawing teeth. She even kept her tinned goods in an old metal fishing box that had once held her father's bobbers and bass plugs. Otherwise, the beasties would chew off the labels, making it impossible to distinguish between the mushroom soup and the chili beans.

While Sheila was appalled at the notion of mice foraging in her pantry, the sight of baby rodents squirming

blindly amid the ruins of their nest was equally disconcerting.

Gabby snapped up two baby mice before she could
grab his collar.

The horror sent Sheila into a frenzy. Flailing a dishtowel, she chased the bewildered beagle into the living
room. Gabby bounded behind the coat rack hung with
colourful raincoats and hats. When it toppled, the dog
was hopelessly enmeshed in Sheila's mosquito bonnet.
After turning the hat into a sort of tutu, Gabby leaped for
the sofa. Sheila managed to swipe her brother's beloved
lawn darts trophy off the fireplace mantel before her
broom found its mark and the dog barrelled through the
screen door.

Three blind mice remained. Not one of them was as
big as Sheila's thumb. Sheila picked up one of the pul-
sating daubs of life and figured that it weighed about as
much as a marshmallow. Its tail was as delicate as angel
hair pasta. Its pink ears were smaller than Rice Krispies.
Then Sheila remembered what Gabby had done and decided to avoid comparing the half-formed mice to any food
product.

Sheila left the nest alone for an hour, hoping that the
mother mouse would return and relocate her family, but
nothing came or went. The babies seemed restless and
their fragmented nest was irreparable. Sheila decided to
make one of her own. Using a powder puff as a base, she
lined a margarine tub with cotton batten. The mouse kin
burrowed into the fluff. Sheila took the margarine tub to
her desk overlooking the lake and turned the gooseneck
reading light on to keep her charges warm.

It was the first day of Sheila's annual vacation at the cottage, two weeks that she set aside purposefully as her annual opportunity to "sit perfectly still," abandoning all thoughts about the personnel placement agency she owned and operated. Now she found herself digging the cellular phone out of her purse and wondering who she could call on a Sunday summer afternoon about the care and feeding of orphan mice.

I picked up the telephone message just before dusk after spending the day rototilling the garden, re-seeding plots of lettuce and spinach and watering transplanted trees. When I heard Sheila's voice, my thoughts turned to blue water, big rocks and the wild blueberries that grow on a hill next to her cottage. The last thing I expected was a poignant voice-mail pleading for a mouse milk formula.

Farmers do not as a rule spend a lot of time hand-raising mice. More frequently, we are plotting their demise. Eradication methods run the gamut from blood-curdling poison to electronic mouse-eardrum-piercing devices. By the time I returned Sheila's phone call she had already been offered the services of two cats and a plastic bag suitable for mouse drowning. Instead, she had driven two hours to town and back to purchase a canned, baby milk substitute, which she was warming as we spoke.

This let me off the hook. My suggestion would have involved milk or cream mixed with an egg for protein, but I held faint hope for the survival of such small, wild creatures. Sheila recognized the caution in my voice, but she just had to try. She had even improvised a "bottle," using a hollowed ballpoint pen with a strip of rubber band fashioned around the nib. Her phone battery was running low, but she promised to call in the morning with preliminary results.

As it turned out, Sheila's "bottle" was a complete flop. The mice were too small and too disoriented to figure out why something so hard was being thrust between their lips. But they were hungry, squeaking and sniffing for something recognizable as a mother.

Sheila ended up holding each one in her left palm while she spooned three or four drops of warm formula into the groove between her index and her forefinger and prodded the little guys to take a sip. Each feeding session took half an hour under the glow of the gooseneck lamp. Sheila was up every four hours throughout the night, doling out the sticky formula which she kept warm in a film canister surrounded by hot water in a tea cup. An apologetic Gabby sat at Sheila's feet, thumping his tail on the hooked rug whenever she cooed, "There's a good mouse."

The absurdity of the situation was not lost on Sheila. She simply could not turn her back on the helpless creatures.

Two of the mice died in the night. Sheila's voice was choked with disappointment when she told me about burying them side by side in a handkerchief underneath a cedar tree behind the cottage.

The sole survivor seemed to have figured out the hows and wheres of eating and Sheila opined that it might have even grown a bit over night. Buoyantly optimistic, she took time between feedings to dash into town and stock up on baby formula, which raised a few eyebrows in the grocery store since everyone on the lake knew that Sheila was a career spinster.

A few curious neighbours drifted to the dockside with the usual invitations and warnings about the latest shallow rocks. Sheila spoke about the plight of the mouse in hushed tones. Coincidentally, one of her fellow cottagers was a cat breeder, who had considerable experience dealing with sickly kittens. On seeing the mouse, she suggested that its round belly might be more than just milk-filled.

She left Sheila with some instructions.

Early in the morning of the third day of her vacation, Sheila found herself listening to the call of a loon while she massaged the tummy of the mouse until it relieved itself on a wad of paper towels. Along with the times and amount of its feedings, Sheila added a column on her notepad devoted to the times and consistencies of such renderings. When we spoke, Sheila confided that she had never aspired to become an oracle of mouse droppings.

Under Sheila's care, the young mouse thrived. By the end of the vacation, its rose-petal skin was picking up a slick of grey-brown hair. Eyes, once tightly shut, now bulged from their sockets. In the morning, when the screen door squeaked open letting Gabby out, the mouse would waken, sometimes sitting on its haunches, wiggling its nose and sniffing out a greeting. The mouse was so small that its sex seemed unknowable, or at least unseeable. Sheila just called it "Sweetie."

On the crawl one night, Sweetie nearly fell off the desk. The next day, Sheila rummaged through the cob webs in the old boathouse and found the aquarium she and her brother had used to contain everything from salamanders to turtles. Mixing shredded newspaper with finely clipped cedar greens she made a mousehouse, complete with a thimble full of milk and a pop bottle cap filled with crumbled granola.

Without the mouse, Sheila's holiday would have been as routine as she always scheduled it to be — clearing rocks and driftwood from the sandy shoreline, painting a couple of chairs, installing new bathroom drapes and taking long walks with Gabby past all of the old familiar trees of her childhood. And she did all those things, along with sitting perfectly still, but this year she did them with the mouse, even devising a carrying case made out of an old jewellery box covered with window screen mesh.

When it was time to lock up the cottage, Sheila left everything as she had found it for her brother and his brood. A few fractures in the lawn dart trophy were barely visible after she glued the parts together. The pantry was secured and there was no sign that the cottage had been used as a nursery for a rodent.

On the drive home, Sheila stopped at a pet store and bought Sweetie a fine hamster cage with all of the trimmings. One was for her home and one was for the office. The mouse went to work with Sheila, sleeping, eating and generally amusing itself under her great wooden desk. When she was alone, Sheila frequently let the mouse roam freely. The mouse became her constant companion and also something of a *scandale.*

From behind the closed door of her office, people passing along the corridor would often hear something they did not put together with Sheila's rather proper image. Things like: "Sweetie, stop that nibbling. I told you not to nibble there." Or "Sweetie, I told you NOT on the desk ever again." People who thought of Sheila as austere and cold, looked at her in a new light.

Sheila never found another mouse at the cottage but she always took Sweetie with her for the annual vacation. I joined her there one afternoon. We ate wild blueberries with cream on the front porch and watched the mouse chase after peanuts with the chipmunks. No mouse ever had it so good.

RECYCLING FISH

Women who fish are treated either as prizes or poisons. If a woman fishes quietly, and does not lose her lure or tangle her line, she may be allowed back in the boat. If a woman does all this and offers to clean the fish of others, she will be given her own life preserver. On the other hand, if a woman offers the opinion "yuck" to anything, from handling live bait leeches to eating sandwiches that were left in the live well, she can be voted off the boat in an instant. Women who can't change their own lures, or who choose lures that are inappropriate to the circumstance, or who insist on casting into areas where they have previously lost lures are pariahs on any fishing boat.

I know because I am a woman who fishes. It took me years to get used to the process of acceptance. Men see a woman with a fishing rod and they automatically get the sort of look on their faces that they had as children when they were told they had to get along with a geeky cousin. Moose has never treated me that way, but then he knows that I pack an excellent lunch and can fillet almost anything.

Being a woman who fishes can anger certain men. I know that I did not impress the fishing guide in Costa Rica when I let out a Tarzan yell in the middle of the jungle. Rivers flowing to the ocean through a tangle of trees covered with slippery green bark and vines were the home of colourful little fish we were supposed to catch with tiny wooden baits. The air smelled of jasmine blossoms and monkeys were screaming in the trees. I could catch a million sunfish in a neigbour's pond that were as pretty as the river fish, but how often does a woman get a chance to render a Tarzan yell in the middle of a real jungle?

Men take fishing quite seriously. They cannot imagine that a woman could possibly take fishing as seriously as they do. So when I joined a convoy of serious muskellunge fishermen on an excursion from Manitoulin Island, through Northern Ontario and on to the Manitoba border, I had to prove myself. Those boys put cherry brandy in their coffee at 6 a.m. and that takes some surviving.

It was October and the weather ranged from freezing rain to balmy sun. We were on big water, unfamiliar water, but one thing fishermen understand is that finding the fish is much more than luck and it has a lot to do with things like "structure." So you can imagine how surprised the boys were when I told them I had been studying charts of the lake and had found some really nice areas where there was rock structure that rose near the surface and then led to a big drop-off. That sort of "structure" close to reedy edgewater where cabbage weed grows was a classic hunting ground for the elusive and huge muskie. I did not catch a big one there, but one of the guys did — right where I thought we might find one.

After that, I was about as close as one could get to being a mascot for the Muskie Maniacs of Manitoulin, led by Muskie Mike of Manitowaning. The ragtag crew of us fished every puddle capable of holding a muskellunge every chance we got. As landlocked as a farmer can become, I will always treasure those days on the water in the wilderness where rainbows could arch from one side of the lake to the other and you did not need a camera to never forget the sight.

Fishing is not an easy business and it becomes exacerbated and positively nerve-wracking when the stakes are higher than a round of drinks. That is perhaps one of the greatest differences between men and women who fish. Women are less likely to gloat in a competitive circumstance. I discovered this during a salmon fishing derby in Lake Huron's Georgian Bay. Big boats, big water and big prizes all for one big fish. The purchasing of a derby ticket seems to be the moment of transformation for most fishermen. The idea that they are investing $25 in order to try to catch a fish that they could also be trying to catch without paying for anything more than their fishing licence seems to create a fervor in their attitude toward what is, after all, an entertainment, a recreation, even a sport.

There were six of us on a 30-foot boat that day. Each person had a designated down-rigger rod set in a holder. The rods were bent down, weighted below the water to pull the silver and blue lures along at prescribed depths that held to prescribed speeds. There were meters that

read the visibility in water at various depths and pre-
dicted the colour of lure that would best be seen by a fish.
There were water temperature gauges and graphs that
charted the bottom and electronic fish finders that
showed bait fish and big fish alike. The only thing missing was an adjustable underwater video camera to mon-
itor the fish avoiding the lures. Yes, such things exist.

We fished hard, starting in the early dawn with
about 600 other boats stretching across Owen Sound har-
bour. There was every type of boat from rafts to yachts.
Small boaters lobbed grapefruits at the big boats that
threatened to wash them over in their wake and the level
of competence of many captains was questionable. A 30-
foot boat starts out seeming like a big deal, but after four
hours and no fish caught, it becomes a bit close.

The good news was that nobody was catching fish.
The professional charter captains were as stymied as the
locals sitting on the dock casting marshmallows. At the
beginning of the morning, people spoke in code over their
marine radios, careful to keep contact only with their bud-
dies. By noon hour, they were swapping old war stories
about all the fish they caught last year and exactly what
lure they had used. Rods were rigged and re-rigged. I
knew the men were thinking that I was the jinx.

I really felt that I was just there because I made the
sandwiches. I had been given an outside line that nobody
gave an outside chance of catching a fish, since it had a
big flashing lure on it that was designed to attract fish to
the "real" lures rather than actually catch a fish. So there
was hell to pay when my rod flipped up and I yelled,
"Fish on!" lurching for the rod and pulling it out of the

cradle while the men watched, their eyes bulging and their mouths pursed. If this fish got away there would be worse than hell to pay.

I will confess to having the odd habit of screaming when I am battling a particularly large fish. So, while the men were reeling in their lines to avoid tangles, I was emitting enough sound to alert the entire bay to the fact that some woman had caught a fish. Boats were soon steering our way, but I could not watch — the fish was playing with me. It was showtime.

Salmon are feisty fish that will do aerial maneuvers, shaking their fish heads, trying to spit the lure out. They pull and they go on runs, stripping line off the reel in a high-pitched zzzzzzz. All the men were providing me with instructions, while they squabbled over who would handle netting the fish. On the radio, people were shouting the question, "How big is it?"

I knew the fish was no derby winner, but I brought it in with all of the skill I had. To lose it would have been to disgrace the whole boat. It weighed 18 pounds, making it a nice fish but nothing near the 30 pounds and up that would win the big prize. As soon as it was landed, the men started getting their lines back in the water. Where there was one fish there was bound to be more. Boats around us were already battling fish and it could have been the beginning of a feeding frenzy. My line was the last one rigged, but I noticed several of the guys had changed over to big clunky lures like mine.

All around us boats began catching fish. The air smelled of salmon. Men were whooping and hollering. One charter captain was having a particularly good day.

After each fish was caught, he would turn on his radio and announce the weight in a steely tenor worthy of Johnny Cash — 16 pounds, 22 pounds, 28 pounds — but none of the rods on our boat were moving. The rest of the day was like that and by sunset the boys were ready to give up. While we took one more pass across Thompson's Hole where the structure was amazing, I decided I would clean my little salmon since there were lineups forming at the fish-cleaning stations beside the dock. I had the fillet stripped off in no time and we tossed the rest in the water. At least everyone would go home with a nice chunk of salmon to show for the day.

I had washed my hands in a bucket of orange-scented water and the men were popping up fishing lines and securing the boat for travel when I saw my rod go off again.

"Fish on!" I yelled.

The battle began. No line sang out but the beast seemed determined to go to the bottom. Fish will do that, hide under the boat and dart from side to side. Fish can confound you into thinking that they are really smart. I gave no quarter, leaning into the fish pulling up and reeling in.

"The rod's going to break," said one of the younger men. And he was right, it was bent clear over but as long as I walked with it I could keep reeling in. Everyone stayed out of my path. There were times when I felt that all I could do was hold the fish steady. No one else could touch the rod or the taking of what was obviously a monstrous trophy fish would not count. We had a sizable crowd around us by now and word had gone out over the radio that "some broad" had a big fish on.

After about 20 minutes, I knew the fish was getting close. The net man was in position and the boat lights were on as we all tried to catch the first glimpse. I got it right to the surface before the horror struck.

There it was in all its glory, the bony carcass of the 18-pound salmon I had filleted that afternoon. I saw the men looking down at it, and then looking up at the boats that bobbed in the near dark waiting to see the net scoop the fish, waiting to hear the whoops of victory.

"She caught the carcass," I heard one of them say under his breath.

"I don't believe it, she caught the first fish again," said another, in a long chuckling wheeze. "She caught the bones, for crying out loud."

"Give me a knife," I said.

For the price of a $10 lure, I saved the dignity of the boat. When the line snapped and the rod straightened out, the men groaned in unison.

"She lost it. It was a monster. Sure winner. Sure winner," shouted the men to all and sundry and it went out over the radio that "the woman" had lost the fish at the last moment. The fish was said to weigh 37 pounds and it had to have been the biggest, thickest salmon any of the men had ever seen.

Back at the dock the condolences never stopped. Each one came with the offer of a libation. If nothing else, not catching fish makes you a cheap date.

FISHING WITH MY BOY WALLY

If there is anything men are more suspect of than a woman who fishes, it is a woman who fishes with her dog. I have fished with everything from a laid-back bull mastiff to a terribly interested Shar-Pei, and I think dogs can enjoy fishing as much as I do.

However, fishing with a bull terrier began as a distinct challenge. We were up on Manitoulin Island in a place I think of as a sort of friendly heaven on earth on its good days. It is a big wilderness island, dotted with cottages on clear, clean lakes.

Most of the dogs I have fished with either went to sleep or knew enough to stand back when someone yelled, "Fish on!" Wally would have nothing of that. He chased his soccer ball along the water's edge until he finally had to be loaded into the boat and strapped into a life preserver.

Moving away from land was an excitement. Initially. Wally wanted to dive into the rooster-tail plume of water churned up by the engine, but he did not like the spray or the wind on his face and finally found a place to lie down amid the tackle boxes.

We cut the engine on the boat near the secret fishing spot and slid into a little bay so quietly that not even the loons took note. Casting for bass in the reeds, we had big jigs rigged on the lines, colourful rubbery things that are supposed to look like something a fish wants to eat. The baits sang out over the water, and Wally sang right after them. He barked loud enough to wake a sleeping mud turtle and bring it to the surface for a look. Every cast prompted a new round of wanton barking. Every fish in the lake headed away from our little boat, far away.

Fed up, I tossed a towel at Wally. It covered his head and he stopped barking. That's when I discovered that as long as a towel loosely covers his head, Wally stays as quiet as a dead parrot.

I do not share these fishing secrets lightly.

KARMA CHAMELEON

Enough time has passed that I think I am ready to let Karma out of the closet. She's a palomino. She's pretty. But she is a horse of specific preference. She only likes members of her own sex. The boy thing she just does not get, and as far as sex itself goes, she hasn't got much use for it in any form. When Mennonites drive their buggies along the fenceline road, Karma's ears perk up when the working horse is female. They flatten back and her eyes turn mean when the horse is male, even though, inevitably, it is a gelding. Her attitude changes in the presence of the opposite sex faster than a chameleon on a crazy quilt. I have no explanation.

It is true that Karma has led a somewhat sheltered life. She was born 17 years ago beside the window in the family room where her pregnant mother, Lady, came to watch television each night. She is the only foal ever born on the farm and, in her entire life, she has never been separated from her mother. She has never shared a pasture with a male of her species.

A few weeks after she was born, it was time for Lady to be re-bred. I was so pleased with the golden foal that I was returning her to the same stallion. Wilmer, the consummate horse trader who sold me on the stallion in the first place, had assured me that I had a good chance of getting another palomino foal from my palomino mare if I used his bay Thoroughbred stud. The horse was handsome and well-tempered.

We were loading Lady and Karma into Ken "Hooter" Houston's horse trailer, when the skittish foal somehow managed to kick Ken in the groin.

Maybe it was a mistake, but Ken didn't think so. Fortunately, he was just grazed

"That filly just doesn't like men," Ken said, when I was able to walk the baby horse quietly into the trailer. One thing Ken knows is the nature of horses.

Lady was not at Wilmer's very long before the deed was done and I got the call to retrieve them. Like a true horse trader, Wilmer insisted on payment right away. I was just glad to have both of them back. If all went well, eleven months later I would have another foal.

After six months I expected to see some changes in Lady's anatomy, but she remained as sleek as a spring muskrat. The vet did an internal exam and discovered that Lady was no more pregnant than I was.

I stopped by Wilmer's to give him the news, but he was away. His stable helper said she would pass the information along. She remembered that mating because it had not gone well. The foal was in a pen bawling and neighing its head off the whole time and the mare could not be settled.

In true horse-trading tradition, I did not get a refund and the stallion had been sold.

Four years passed and I decided to try again, this time breeding both horses. Karma had matured, but she still resisted any attempt to remove her from her mother's sight. With me, she was playful and well-behaved, if somewhat spoiled. She would nip at Moose, and turn her backside toward him threateningly. He was always a bit nervous around her, having witnessed the groin-hoofing Hooter took. I hoped a foal of her own would mellow her and I found a stylish and well-bred quarter horse stallion nearby. He was a chestnut, but I was assured that he had sired palominos in the past. Payment, as usual, was in advance.

The horses stayed at the breeding stable for three weeks, until I got an angry call from the owner telling me to come and get my horses. I knew that the first breeding had not gone well. While Lady was in the breeding shed "standing" as the mare is supposed to do, Karma had jumped a fence and taken a few runs through the various barns hysterically searching for her mommy. This unsettled the process. When it was Karma's turn, the romantic moment was foiled when she repeatedly kicked out at the stallion and refused to quiet down.

The breeder decided to wait for a second try, after allowing the horses to become more familiar with their surroundings. But the second try had been even more disastrous. This time Karma was locked in a stall while her mother went off for her date. Apparently, Karma screamed louder than a braying mule, causing her mother to lose that loving feeling and dampening the ardour of the stud horse. Karma herself was hobbled for the event, a procedure I might not have allowed had I known about it. Nevertheless she managed to break free, destroying a halter and inflicting a bite on the stallion that required eleven stitches.

I did not get a refund. I was lucky I did not get shot.

"Your mare has a sexual-identity problem," the breeder said. Other descriptives were added; the same sort Hooter used when Karma kicked him.

Karma and Lady are now both past the breeding phase of their lives. They spend their time together and rarely quarrel over anything except food. A dotty old mother and her equally dotty old daughter, they stand at the fenceline that overlooks the road — watching all the girls go by.

THE GARBAGE GESTAPO

We call the guys who manage the dump "the Garbage Gestapo." Their official designation is probably something like "waste management site supervisors" or "environmental land fill engineers."

There is a gate on the dump these days to stop folks from dumping their garbage when there is no one to keep an eye on them. And there is adequately spelled signage, directing the path for dumping household waste, recyclables, metal, tires, poisons and toxins. At great expense, a truck-sized weigh scale greets each citizen and their garbage, along with a "STOP" sign so that you can gather your senses and decide whether to weigh your garbage and pay by the pound or just declare the number of bags you've accumulated and pay the dump collectors their tithe.

Before the township started charging its citizens a dollar a bag to dump their garbage, there was just "Charlie." Sometimes Charlie drove the backhoe, pushing and rolling the garbage into huge mounds where the seagulls clustered like dandruff. And sometimes Charlie just sat in the backhoe seat with the windows open and the radio on, surveying the garbage for signs of what, we did not know. Dump cats came and went, usually leaving a fresh litter of dump kitties behind them.

In those days, if you were bringing anything that you thought might have value or meaning to someone else, you just dropped it off at the side of the pile with the other old lamp stands, bent-door refrigerators, rusty bedsprings and kicked-in television sets. Sometimes folks left the dump with more stuff than they came in with. In a pinch, you could always find an odd piece of scrap metal or lumber at the dump. Nobody thought any less of you for taking home a three-legged chair and fixing it up. And nobody counted you a failure if the same chair showed up a few months later with the same leg still missing.

People can still leave semi-useful stuff at the dump, but they have to put it in the right pile. Metal goes with metal, meaning everything from old bicycles to leaky water heaters is lumped together. Old sofas are considered "household waste," and anything made of wood, from cracked window frames to old barn doors ends up next to the brush pile beside the forest. Leftover paint, worn-out batteries and unreliable barbeque tanks are all organized in a building of their own. The days of one-stop shopping at the dump are over.

Organizing the dump created its own havoc. In fact, any change at the dump always seems to upset the unnatural balance of the place. A picture of a scrubby-looking dump cat in the local paper prompted a spate of adoptions. This was well and good, but while the pampered dump cats dined on Tender Vittles in their new homes, the rat population at the dump grew in leaps and bounds.

When a picture of rats overrunning the dump, snoozing on abandoned sofas and using piles of tires as their personal jungle gym appeared in the local paper, nobody rushed out to adopt them. Instead, the local television station was called in to capture the full effect of seething hordes of rats descending on fresh garbage. The rats didn't look scrubby at all — in fact, they were fine, big sleek rats and the sight of hundreds of them swarming what looked like the leftovers from the Kinsmen's barbeque was most disconcerting on the 6 o'clock news.

Poisoning the rats seemed like a good idea, until several sharp eyes spotted a few fat dump kitties still at large. Old-timers in town recalled the days when Fridays were "good ol' boy" nights at the dump and they would grab a case of "pop" and wile away the dusk shooting rats for target practice.

The idea of a rat shoot at the dump was appealing to some, although they knew enough to keep such a notion confined to their sheds and truck cabs. Bleeding hearts and politicians who thought about things like municipal insurance could pose a problem. So one Friday night, the boys just loaded up and drove a few trucks out into the cornfield behind the dump and scaled the chain-link fence, leaving two guys with hip replacements behind to keep watch.

The banging and whooping lasted about 45 minutes before police cars convened at the front gate of the dump.

The last of the rat hunters was long gone by the time the rat busters got Charlie out to open the locked gate. Apparently, there was some carnage but no signs of a massive massacre. A lot of garbage bags were shot clean through, and a large number of glass and tin recyclables were scattered near the back fence.

Charlie was instructed to bulldoze the whole open pit and cover it with fresh earth. Soon neighbouring farmers were scrambling to adopt the progeny of dump cats to keep up with the rats that spread out in search of food and took refuge in their granaries. Life at the dump is never boring.

At the new-fangled dump, the citizens are not supposed to pick around for "good stuff," but that is a joke. One poor municipal planner actually told a public meeting that people would not be allowed to remove discarded bicycles and such for parts. That was tantamount to a challenge. What was the Garbage Gestapo going to do, inspect every vehicle that left the dump for signs of outgoing garbage? And were they going to charge for that?

The fact is that many people consider one person's cast-offs found treasure. In fact, when "good stuff" began disappearing from the dump, there was a quiet public outcry in the coffee shop and some internal investigation was conducted at the dump. Sure enough, one of the Garbage Gestapo was discovered to be scavenging the best stuff for himself. Then it would end up with a "for sale" sign on it at the end of his lane and somebody who could have picked up, say, a busted lawn mower, for free at the dump would end up spending $10 for the same disappointment. Such behaviour is a firing offence. What is worse, this same purveyor of abandoned goods had the audacity to jump the line, taking "good stuff" that his supervisor should have had dibs on. Tsk. Tsk.

Charging citizens a dollar a bag to receive their garbage was another upset to the natural balance of the dump. The idea was a "green" thinking notion, as well as just another way for local government to gouge the taxpayers. One theory was that if people had to pay for dumping a bag of garbage, they would be more careful about what they put in the bag and practise better recycling habits. That theory worked so well on some citizens that they went to the municipal office to get a second recycling box. Then local government discovered that they were losing money by supplying recycling boxes for free so they started charging $5 for a second recycling box. Of course, this did not work very well, because they could not prove decisively that a person already had one recycling box to begin with. Damaged boxes were supposed to be replaced for free, but did that mean a citizen had to surrender the wrecked box in order to qualify for a free replacement? This prompted visions of a huge pile of gnarly recycling boxes in the parking lot of the municipal offices next to the reeve's new pickup. And they had no rules in place to arbitrate what would happen in the case of a divorce. It was quite a mess.

The bag-for-a-buck thing was also destined for failure. One of the first things people did was figure out that garbage bags come in various sizes. Those big orange bags that are used for leaf collection in the fall could hold two regular-sized green garbage bags. Then some clever soul discovered that the heavy-gauge plastic garbage bags used by contractors could hold a trio of seven-year-olds, or as many as four loosely packed green bags. People started showing up at the dump with just one of these monsters bulging out of their trunk.

"One bag," they would say with a grin, tossing a loonie at the stunned on-duty Garbage Gestapo. Whoever said that size doesn't matter never went to a pay-per-bag dump.

In the towns where garbage collection was provided at curbside the municipality wanted to charge $1.75 per bag. And there was no way out of paying the fee, because the only garbage that the municipality would collect would be in yellow bags that they were selling for $1.75 a piece. This is the kind of arbitrary demand that brings out the same sort of attitude as a bad call by a hockey referee.

Garbage is a personal thing — no one wanted to be told what colour bag they had to use. Lots of people had scores of green garbage bags still in their package. What was to become of those useless bags now? The yellow bags were roomy, which was fine for some, but others preferred a smaller bag. And paying $1.75 to have worn plastic wrap and plate scrapings hauled off . . . whoever heard of such a thing? In the space of four weeks, an anti-user-fee petition circulated in just one of the affected towns and had 1,539 signatures.

The man who put the petition together proudly presented it to county council with the tribute, "You screwed up royally."

The mayor thanked the petitioner, but offered no resolution, saying "We're beyond change."

Not to be considered inflexible, one of the council-lors noted brightly that "Change is progress."

In an attempt to divert attention from the issue at hand, another councillor proposed a half-bag fee for senior citizens who could not come up with a full bag of garbage every week. There was also concern expressed about garbage that was being dumped anonymously in green bags left in ditches and on roadways. Road crews were doing the pickup of what was dubbed "roadkill garbage." To complicate matters, it was costing the municipality $1 a bag to have the road crews dump the garbage that they were retrieving. In another community, someone had counted 15 pizza boxes blowing around town. This was a problem that was not going to go away.

Despite public protest, the public lost. Some council-lors admitted that they felt "caught in the middle" when it came to crucial issues such as whether or not citizens should be allowed to put their user-paid garbage bags inside of garbage tins to prevent animals from ripping them apart. The engineering services chairman warned that pulling garbage bags out of garbage cans can cause back injuries and, besides, the municipality had not received any complaints about dogs destroying garbage bags. Frankly, flying pizza boxes were of more concern, so the council decided to watch and wait on the issue of garbage cans.

One local newspaper, the *Wellington Advertiser*, cov-ered the garbage issue closely, sensing its importance to the grassroots readership. With certain glee it was an-nounced in a front-page story that: "County councillors here spent fewer than ten minutes to pass a budget with expenditures of $117.2 million, but they took up over 70 minutes arguing about the $1.75 fee for garbage pickup, and other issues related to garbage." An editorial columnist made copious reference to "bureaucratic stupidity," and suggested that those persons in charge of explaining the county's rights and responsibilities as far as garbage is concerned should "Get a life!"

Politicians and planners can posture and pose as much as they want to about waste management, but garbage is still garbage and it will not just go away no matter how much is charged to keep it out of sight. Sometimes I think that a day at the dump with the rats, the cats and the seagulls might benefit all of those who choose to filibuster on the topic. At least they should know the sort of Gestapo they create.

FRED'S WAR

There is a sort of war going on at Fred's farm. It's a war between Fred and his dad that started almost as soon as Fred bought the 100-acre farm. And it is kind of a strange war, since Fred bought the farm specifically so that his aging dad would have some place to live until he dies.

Fred visits the farm on weekends, but his dad lives there full time. So there is also a sort of part-time war between two grown men who are at fundamental odds about what a farm should be.

The property itself is the kind that real estate agents like to call "fixer-uppers." The white clapboard house needs a new front porch and wind whistles through most of the windows. The south side of the roof leaks a bit and the basement is a mud bath after a heavy rain. Fred has a list of "things to do" and he is methodical about making improvements.

Fred's dad, on the other hand, thinks the house is just fine. He only uses the kitchen and a few other rooms. Besides, Dad spends most of his time on the road finding things to bring back to the farm because they "still have some use in them." This includes everything from geriatric goats to rusted-out school buses and discarded wood pallets.

And that's what has caused the war.

It started innocently enough when Fred was helping his dad move to the farm. They had lost touch over the years. His dad was living in Winnipeg in the bungalow he had shared with Fred's mom ever since they came from the "Old Country." It was her death that brought the two together again.

Still, Fred had trouble moving his father to the farm. Everything in the old bungalow seemed to have sentimental value.

"We used that icebox back in the fifties and it still works," the old man said.

And so it had to go on the truck.

Fred finally gave up sorting the treasures from the dross and loaded the whole kit and caboodle on the moving truck. Consequently, most of the rooms at the farmhouse that Fred's dad doesn't use are filled with unpacked boxes from the old house. Every time Fred opens an upstairs bedroom door, he lets out a long sigh.

Getting the pickup truck might have been Fred's second mistake. He thought a farm needed a truck and his dad could use it to get to town for supplies. But what Fred's dad used the truck for was another thing. He used it to go to the dump, not to take the garbage, rather to pick through garbage for "good stuff."

A farm would not be a farm without livestock. So, every once in a while Dad salvaged a living thing at a neigbour's or a farmers' market. Dad brought home kittens and broken-down dogs, orphan ducklings, hens that refused to lay and mean geese that hissed.

Even a billy goat that was too smelly for someone else to manage was no problem for Dad to load into the king cab of the truck and haul home. And there's no point in having a billy if you don't have a nanny goat — so soon there was a goat herd grazing in Fred's carefully planted vegetable garden.

At first, Fred's dad tried to hide the "stuff" he gathered, depositing the old pails, worn-out water heaters and worse-for-wear window frames along the back-forty fenceline. Of course, Fred would find every new deposit on his weekend walks in search of predators whom he suspected were killing the cats his father kept "finding." In fact, Fred's dad was hiding the cats in the barn granary and feeding them buckets of goat milk.

But Oscar the billy goat was never a secret. He has a tinkling bell on a dog collar strapped to his neck, and anyone with a nose knows when Oscar is near. The pungent scent of goat that emanates from a gland just behind Oscar's curved horns is worse than ripe Limburger cheese.

Big white Oscar comes to the kitchen door in the morning, bangs it open with his head and goes directly to the pantry where Fred's dad keeps cartons full of "perfectly good" lettuce and other vegetables the local supermarket was planning to throw out. No one argues with Oscar. Yelling at him might provoke a billy run through the whole house. Better to allow Oscar to chew his greens in peace and waddle back to the barnyard where he curls up next to a pile of old tires and basks in the sun.

After a year and half, almost a third of the 100 acres on the farm bore some mark of the scavenger father. Half-wrecked lawn chairs sprouted all over the front lawn, next to a stash of aged lawn mowers that all just needed a part — or 12.

Fred took pictures of the goats standing on the old vehicles that had collected near the woodlot. The goats used the rusted hoods and machine parts to stand on while they stripped the young trees of bark and leaves.

Fred determined that goats are happiest when they can combine their two favourite activities — jumping to climb trees and eating to kill trees. His dad said they were "foraging."

Still, even Fred admits that baby goats are cute. The long-eared goat kids navigate their way over and around metal culverts Fred's dad has "imported" for them to play on. And the nanny goats lounge on a well-worn three-seater sofa, grazing on whatever it was that had been stuffed in the pink-and-green floral cushions.

Looking around one fine spring day, Fred lost it. He laid down the law and managed to get his dad to help him take four pickup truck-loads of junk to the dump. The haul included: four fridges, five stoves, one freezer, two washing machines, one oil furnace and lots of chairs. A mere dint, but Fred thought it was a start.

The next weekend, Fred returned to discover that his dad had begun re-stocking, including bringing back from the dump one old washing machine that was now even more battered than it had been the previous weekend.

"You said the old things had to go, but when I bring them back they're new," said Dad.

Fred started giving up the battle slowly.

To protect the "stuff" his dad insisted on stacking like hay bales in the barn, Fred went to work installing big new barn doors.

Although his dad's only job was to hold the ladder and call 911 if Fred fell, one nimble goat made it halfway up the ladder before Fred could get his dad's attention.

Fred loves the farm pond, but his dad has populated it with a flock of ducks who quack wildly any time Fred goes near the water. So Fred plans to dig his own pond. And he plans to salvage some of the goat-eaten cedars and turn them into poles to form a fence around "his" pond.

And Fred has installed locks on a couple of the rooms in the farmhouse. Every time he leaves, Fred takes a few boxes with him. Soon he figures one room at least will be cleared out and he might be able to make it into a guest room.

None of Fred's plans escape his father's watchful eye. Dad has already told Fred that he's made a few friends who wouldn't mind coming to stay and visit for a while if they had a spare bedroom. Fred figured that wasn't far off when he saw that his dad had begun collecting discarded bed frames from the dump.

The war between Fred and his father is fought *mano a mano*, metre by metre every inch of the way on the farm. It is a private war. His dad fires a salvo, literally a kitchen sink here and another there. Fred replies by removing all the junk around the well pump and installing a new concrete pad.

It will take a lifetime to turn Fred's farm into a thing of beauty. And that's just what he had in mind when he bought the farm, where his dad will live until he dies. They would not be happy together unless they had some battle on the boil.

"You'd be amazed at how much trouble one old man can get up to," says Fred.

"He's stubborn, my son," says Fred's dad, with just the tiniest hint of pride.

"JUST STUFF"

Someone out there has a picture of me with a very large fish. The fish is a muskellunge. At about 30 pounds, it's a whopping big muskie. I caught the brute at a top secret lake on Manitoulin Island last summer. Moose took the photo from the other end of the boat. The shutter snapped and then I lowered the big fish into the water and cradled her in my arms. When she was ready, the fish flipped her tail and swam away.

I bet it's a great picture. I was so happy to have finally caught a fish I could be proud of and then return it to the lake in truly sporting fashion. But I don't think I'll ever see that photograph, because it was in the camera that was stolen.

Stolen, oh yes, indeed. The farm was burglarized.

It happened around Thanksgiving, when Moose and I were off in the splendid wilderness of Cape Breton. In fact, the police have narrowed the time period to the Saturday of Thanksgiving weekend. Probably at night. Which means that while the Moose and I were tapping our toes in the Red Shoe Pub to the Celtic accordion styling of Newfoundland's Bernard Felix in a coastal village called Mabou, some jerks were carting away all of the electronics and stereo equipment in our house 2,000 kilometres away.

We found out about the robbery soon after it happened. Friends from Toronto were scheduled to stay at the farm during Thanksgiving, as they have every Thanksgiving for the past decade when a group of us gather to share the spirit of the harvest season. Harvey and Sandra had directions to find the front-door key, but they didn't need one. The door was already open.

They found the house in a state of disarray that was beyond the normal state of my cluttered housekeeping. And then they started noticing that things were missing — things like televisions and stereos and such.

Moose and I were sitting at the cottage we'd rented in Baddeck, overlooking Bras d'Or Lake and the stately grounds of the Cape Breton summer home that Alexander Graham Bell called *Beinn Bhreagh*, Gaelic for "Beautiful Mountain." It was a sparkling morning that ran from deep blue water to the splash of autumn leaves. Then the cell phone rang and it was Harvey, gently inquiring as to the possible whereabouts of certain household items, like the 36-inch television that he thought he remembered seeing in the family room.

And there it was, that sinking long-distance feeling you get when you are far from home and something has gone awry which you have no control over.

So instead of heading up the Cabot Trail on that picture-perfect day, we squatted in the cottage racking up long-distance phone calls to the police and the insurance adjustor.

Logic does not prevail at such times. We sent Harvey and Sandra on scouting missions to check on certain things we treasure.

Yes, all the sheep were in their field. So were the horses.

But no, there was no computer in the downstairs office.

The CDs were in their place — the jazz, the Sinatra, the Elvis — but the CD player was gone. Perhaps the thieves were Aerosmith fans.

And outside the house, under an old lilac bush, two aged televisions were nestled under the guest-room duvet — rejected by the thieves. Not quite up to their standards, I suppose.

After a few phone calls, we deduced that a considerable haul of stuff was missing. But the things we really value, books, heirlooms, antiques and the familiar objects that make a house a home were all intact. The police were called and they determined that the theft had been relatively recent, basing their theory on the freshness of the tire tracks on the front lawn and the moisture content in the abandoned duvet. A stepladder, caked mud and a broken window latch provided the theory of entry.

So the "When" and the "Where" of the case was solved, but not the "Who" and the sum of exactly "What" had to wait until we returned home and took a complete inventory.

"Why" is one of those imponderables that resides in the answer to the question "Who." But since there was no malicious damage — none of the wanton savagery, like urination, defecation and willful breakage so often associated with such burglaries — the violation factor was not as high as it could have been. Just stuff.

I was pondering that while I sat in the Cape Breton cottage, watching a big Love Boat–type cruise ship cross Bras d'Or Lake heading for Baddeck.

One person's stuff can also be another person's livelihood or dreamscape. The downstairs computer was the Moose's new plaything. And, probably because it was new, he had been attentive to details, like backing up the material he had been working on and keeping separate copies of hideous things like accounts payable.

But my old reliable computer in the upstairs office next to my library, well, I have not been as serious as I should be about ensuring the safety of all the information stored in that funky computer brain. Research material, partially completed stories, ideas for stories and all the farm records were stored there, along with all the letters I have written to friends over the years. I tried to look on the bright side.

Thank goodness, all my book manuscripts were stored somewhere else. Thank goodness, I had printed out a draft of my new manuscript and taken it with me. Thank goodness, old ideas that were good enough for me to ponder the first time seem to drift around in my brain endlessly waiting for me to return to them.

My thoughts were beginning to stray from the bright side when the police officer called on the cell phone. He confirmed many things were gone and discussed his theory of the crime.

"Looks like they only took the newest things. Stuff they know has a market," he said. "For instance, I'm up here in a room with a bunch of books and there's a stereo receiver but it looks like whatever was on the shelf above it is gone."

"That would be my office and my television," I told him. "The TV was barely a year old and hardly used. But I have had that Kenwood stereo receiver tuned to CBC Radio for 22 years. It's old but it works."

"Yeah, yeah," said the police officer, "and I guess they didn't want this old computer system here either."

And suddenly I felt better than any honeymooner on any Love Boat cruise to Cape Breton. I felt like an old friend had walked back into my life after a near-death experience. Age may have wearied the marketability of my computer, but age also saved it. I guess that means that even if I had been home when the thieves arrived, they wouldn't have bothered to take me.

So in the end, all I lost was "just stuff."

And anyone who's thinking of trying it again should think twice, because Moose commanded the installation of all manner of surveillance and security device. He's even contemplating training the sheep to attack the unwelcome.

I still hate the idea that some strange, corrupted thieves out there held the camera that holds the undeveloped film with the photograph of me and my big fish. And I'm not holding my breath thinking that I will ever get it back. But if some friendly stranger out there happens upon a bargain in a gently used Nikon at a flea market or something, and you happen to find a roll of film in

there and you have it processed and discover a picture of
a middle-aged woman in a boat holding a fish that probably weighs more like 20 pounds than the 30 pounds she
tells everyone it weighed — could you please just send it
to me — no questions asked.

THE CAMERON FENCE

There is an old rural saying that says: "Build one new fence every year, and you will not have to build all new fences one year."

This is very good advice, but like much good advice it is often ignored or put off until the next year.

When I bought my farm it had no fences to speak of, at least none that worked. Ancient cedar rail fencing around the perimeter had fallen down and was overgrown by vines and brush. Resurrecting the rails seemed impossible, but I salvaged some to make a decorative fence around the barnyard. The age of the yellow-brick farmhouse and the surrounding forest seemed a natural fit with the rugged beauty of cedar rails that had been split and dried by pioneers more than one hundred years earlier.

The fellow who built my first cedar rail fence didn't have much use for them. He was used to planting posts and stretching rolls of page-wire fencing in straight lines. Still, I liked the look of the rail fences, even when I was watching sheep jump over them. Every spring those fences had to be patched. It came to be that they were more of a nuisance than a thing of beauty.

Then Don Cameron came to the farm. Don is a spry, compact man, who wears a peaked cap above his bright blue eyes. He was highly recommended as a man who knows wood.

Trees have grown thick and tall in the 20-acre evergreen stand on the farm. Forest managers have come and gone, rendering plans for thinning and logging the bush to maximize profit in straight, deadly clear-cut rows through the forest. Practical, perhaps, but far too clinical an assault on the forest for my liking.

Moose and I spent half a day walking through the trees with Don and we watched as he fell in love with the forest the same way that we have over the years.

Oh yes, there were trees to be cut. Trees with damaged tops and trees that should come out to allow others to mature properly and let some sunlight in so that new seedlings can take root. But Don envisioned the cutting pattern as more of a path through the trees, a path that would be covered with wood chips. He could trim the lower branches of the trees so that you could ride a horse through the forest. He could build log benches along the way. That would be nice.

Don spent a good month working in the forest. All by himself, he cut trees, trimmed brush and chopped branches into mounds of fragrant chips. Each day, he stopped in the lane and reported on his progress, with a gentle smile.

"There are some good trees in there," he would say, and it felt as though he had been out there patting the bark the way a cowboy pats his horse's neck after a long ride.

One day, Don stopped in the laneway before disappearing into the woods. Moose was trying to repair the cedar rail fence.

"I could fix that fence so it never shifts and even a big bull couldn't get over it," Don said.

Intrigued, we asked what kind of fence he was talking about. The cedar rail fence is a sort of art form, some of them zigzag, some of them are straight lines, some are wired in place and others interlock, but what Don was talking about was his own design, "The Cameron Fence."

It took Don half a day to demonstrate the process. Sheep and horses were moved from the field and the old cedar rail fence around the barnyard came down. Braces for the new fence rose like teepees planted on the ground, not in it, so that they would "float" with natural shifts in the surface.

Small pieces of rail braced the long poles, which were wired in place and reinforced by a side rail across the front. This was no namby-pamby, four-rail-high fence. Each panel of the Cameron Fence consumed a minimum of ten, 12-foot cedar rails. The finished fence was as tall as me. Don stood on the top rails to trim the support teepees and the rails did not so much as quiver.

Just a touch of Cameron Fence was not enough. A rough area of rocky ground where fences had never been stable was perfectly suited to such a freestanding, sturdy fence and I pictured gorgeous, weathered cedar rails lining the laneway and embracing my garden.

While Don was in the forest creating open spaces in the trees, Moose and I were off retrieving cedar rails from our fallen-down fencelines.

We hacked our way through brush and brambles, cursing the idiots who had used barbed wire and long spiked nails to attempt "quick" fixes to the fence.

Pickup loads of cedar rails were hauled back to the farmyard. Some were great huge poles and others were lean, twisted, knotty rails. We lay them in piles along the edges of the 20-year-old page-wire fence, which had begun sagging and threatening to keel over. Don would build the Cameron Fence over the old ones, incorporating the wire for even greater predator protection and eliminating the need to uproot anything that was already there.

Soon the Cameron Fence began to rise around the farm. First along the little orchard pasture outside of the kitchen window where the horses like to graze. Then down the lane and around my garden and off over the rocky promontory.

The fence grew as quickly as we could supply rails. Don was all smiles, even when he was working in a heat wave that sent my animals scurrying for shade.

It's a good thing to see a person who is happy in their work. Years ago, Don laboured in an industrial factory. All sorts of minor ailments befell him, until he finally had to find a new career path. In forests and in working with wood, he found what he needed. All of his work is done outdoors.

And there is an intrinsic honesty to Don's craftsman-ship that reflects the man's philosophy. Nothing is wasted.

Broken rails and stakes find a place in the fence, and the trimmings are piled neatly for kindling. All of the dying or dangerous trees he has removed from the forest have been cut and split for winter burning.

The cherry, poplar, maple and elm make a nice cold weather mix. As an added bonus, I have discovered that firewood stacks perfectly against the wide brace of the Cameron Fence.

But supplying enough rails to keep Don building became a challenge. Once we had depleted our considerable supply, we discovered that commercial vendors and landscape centres wanted anywhere from $2.75 to $6.00 for a single cedar rail. What makes them valuable is the fact that there just aren't any pioneers around making them anymore. Years ago, the government actually gave out grants for page-wire fencing, and in the process many rail fences were ripped out and burned. Now, when I drive by farms and see dilapidated rail fences, I wonder if the farmer knows what precious treasure is melting into the landscape.

One day, on a tour of the side roads, we hit the jackpot. A stack of rails, neatly piled next to the roadway. We bought every last one of them in a flat-rate cash deal that took about three minutes to execute before the usual gossip. And the Cameron Fence kept rising.

People marvel at the rustic, sturdy fence. Don showed it to his mother and she suggested various flowering vines to grace the wood. Birdhouses and feeders perch on the high posts and the winter wood has never looked so organized.

Behind the fence, the sheep are stymied. Horse eyes peer over it and all the animals appreciate its shade. When the guinea fowl begin cackling at dawn, they are perched on the fence facing the rising sun.

Any cedar rail fence is an antique composition. The untreated, sun-dried wooden rails have already lasted longer than any pressure-treated wooden deck ever will. Rescued and recycled, the same planks of split cedar that made so many good neighbours so long ago, can serve the same purpose again.

And rail fencing is so much more interesting to look at than strands of electric wire or straight wooden boards or metal. Don Cameron says that if I string some rope along between the high support rails it will attract squirrels and I can watch them play all winter long.

In spring, the bluebird boxes will welcome song birds and the clematis vines will creep along the rails until they burst into bloom. I think a planting of hollyhocks would suit the fence, and borders of sunflowers, maybe climbing roses.

There is more fence to build so I will be salvaging and hunting out cedar rails throughout the autumn. As I drive along country roads now, I notice each and every rail fence along the way and my "rail radar" is always on alert.

If I could have a new Cameron Fence every year, I would be happy.

The fence is that odd sort of reminder of mortality.

Its materials are older than I am and its construction may well outlast me. At least, I know that with such good fences, there will never come a year when I have to rebuild all of them.

SMALL-TOWN NEWS

Small towns do not like their news to be public. News is something that belongs in the coffee shop and it should not be printed and distributed for all to see. At least, that is the way things often seem the first time you pick up a newspaper from a small town. It takes years to learn to read between the lines, and even more years to be named in an actual line of the paper. Until my picture appeared on the front page of my local paper proudly displaying a set of quadruplet lambs, I thought small-town newspapers were fairly desperate for news.

You will read the darndest things in small-town papers. The first winter I spent on the farm had some terrible storms. Roads were closed around the town and people who were trapped in their cars had to be rescued and brought into town to stay over night. You would think a story that had such human interest would dominate the front page. Instead, it was reported on the front page that storm-stayed strangers stole an ashtray and a towel from the local motel. I was amazed, particularly when it was reported six months later that the ash tray and the towel had been recovered.

There are things that go on in small towns that the residents just don't want public, and it offends their sensibilities when the topic is broached by outsiders. In one small town I know of, there was a local character who lived year-round in a hole in the ground where the house he lived in had once stood. Stories varied, but it seemed the house had burned down and the man had just stayed on, living in the hole, cooking in the hole and sleeping in the remains of the basement. He kept to himself and bothered no one.

This seemed to strike a big-city reporter as newsworthy, so a story was written, although she never gained actual entry to the hole and there were no quotes from the man himself. The mayor told the reporter the man paid his property taxes, which was a part of the public record and just about all she needed to know. There was also some discussion about the fact that the man used public facilities to shower and such. Local high-school students were known to take Christmas dinner to the man who lived in the hole.

There was some uproar when the article appeared. Letters to the editor flew fast and furious, the general consensus being that no outsider had the right to walk into town and think that they could write a story about a man living in a hole without knowing the whole story. One other thing was also certain, nobody from "away" was ever going to know the whole story. To some, the article made it appear that the man was doing something wrong, but it was his hole and he had lived in it for years and everyone knew to keep an eye open for him. It was not as though it was the job of the townsfolk to tell someone who grew up in the town that they could not live in a hole. Some people did wonder if there wasn't some bylaw or building code infringement that could be applied to future cases in which people tried to hole up, but no one thought it necessary to arbitrarily change the living conditions of the current man living in a hole. There has not been a city reporter visit to the town since. At least, not one who was allowed to stay.

Small-town news does not seem like news at all sometimes. It is a matter of who visited with who and who had a baby and who had a funeral: friendships, life and death, just the usual stuff. The politics that creep in are never as juicy as the stories of real chicanery, graft and closed-door dealings that are discussed in the coffee shop. I knew about a steamy love affair between a politician and a town clerk months before it hit the papers, but if you knew what to look for and you read between the lines, you could have guessed as much. That is part of the charm of small-town newspapers. That and the fact that they rarely spell your name the same way twice until you've lived there long enough to earn an obituary.

POLICE BEAT

Speeder of the Week

On August 1, OPP Constable Joe Evans charged two drivers who earned the dubious distinction of being Speeder of the Week in Wellington County.

OPP Constable Keith Robb reported Evans saw two vehicles on County Road 7 appearing to be racing. He paced them at speeds of 170 km/hr in an 80 km zone.

Robb said Evans was able to stop both vehicles, whose drivers said they were in a hurry to get to a bar before it closed.

Source: *Wellington Advertiser*, August 2001

• • • • •

MAN PINNED

An officer patrolling on Highway 89 observed a man pinned under a 14 horsepower riding lawn mower in the ditch at 2:15 a.m.

It is believed the man was trapped for an hour before being rescued.

His reason for driving in the ditch isn't known as he wasn't cutting grass.

Source: *Wellington Advertiser*, April 2000

● ● ● ● ●

NUDE MAN STANDS BY WHILE
WOMAN WAITS FOR TOW

Police are searching for a man who stopped near a vehicle in the ditch here and proceeded to parade around naked in front of the female driver. OPP Constable Dale Gear said the woman drove into the ditch on February 19 because of poor road conditions on County Road 125, south of Brisbane. Gear said that as the woman sat in her car waiting for a tow, a white van pulled up and a male got out and stood beside his vehicle, totally naked. The woman told police the man stood there for about 30 seconds, posing, and then drove away. Gear added that the woman was unable to provide a good description, and police can understand why.

Source: *Wellington Advertiser*, February 2001

LUNCH THEFT

A Mount Forest man was arrested after an armed robbery at the local Becker's store. The thief took a bag from the store clerk as she closed for the night. It turned out to contain the remains of her lunch rather than the day's money.

Source: *The Mount Forest Olds Magazine,*
September 2001, reporting on a 1981 incident.

AGE IN A VACUUM

There are moments in life that seem to identify a binding transition from one phase to another. These are highly personal things that can't be institutionalized or labelled. For instance, in my own personal mythology, I did not become an "adult" until I was 25. By then I was already paying taxes, working responsibly, living alone, winnowing romances and caring for a cat. However, my defining act of becoming an adult was walking into an appliance store and buying a brand new vacuum.

In that moment the things of childhood were shed. No more cast-off cleaning aids from parents and aunts. I had my own spanking new monster — picked by me, paid for by me and lugged home in a taxi by me. I had committed to banishing my own dust bunnies. Adulthood.

I was proud of my new vacuum, but I didn't like it. It was not aesthetically pleasing and the light on its roaring power head scared my cat. Lurking, coiled in a closet, it banished more fanciful items, like high heels and free-weight dumbbells to organized spaces on shelves and hooks.

There were no happy times with the new vacuum, unless you count the initial wonder that comes when you press the "cord retract" button and watch as 28 feet of grey vinyl is slurped into the hard-plastic bowels with lizardly lightning speed. And I thought, "Where does it go? How does it know to do that? Thank God, it's over for another week. Please, cat, forgive the intrusion. It's an adult thing."

My inner child has always taken great pleasure at watching the foibles of my outer adult. Oh how she laughed every time the vacuum hose got plugged. And what a deliciously mature outpouring of gerundized verbs I chose every time I straightened a coat hangar and jammed it recklessly down the hose in search of the source of the clog — one nylon knee-high, three fallen makeup pads, two bobby pins and a catnip toy shaped like a mouse. No dust bunnies, just the detritus of my own hapless life, gobbed up in the symbol of my adulthood.

My vacuum stubbornly denied the aging process. When a crack appeared in the stomach of the machine, I presumed the wound was mortal, but I patched it with duct tape just the same. Five years later, I replaced the duct tape. The machine just kept on hoovering.

Cleaning the farmhouse presented new challenges to my old vacuum cleaner. There were cobwebs in the corners and fly carcasses on window ledges. Dogs track in all manner of muck and somehow I always manage to bring in a trace amount of sheep feed on my clothes. In spring, there are bits of egg shell around the incubator. In summer, clods of dirt from the garden drop from fresh carrots as they are carried to the kitchen sink. Autumn is the time for accidentally spilling pickling spices on the kitchen floor and there are always stray ashes around the wood stove in winter. City vacuums have it easy compared to country vacuums.

My faithful dirt-sucker finally called it quits one day. I hauled it off to the dump, where I expect it was picked over for usable attachments. The hose was still in very good condition for such an old machine. I remember thinking that, as I drove away. The old vacuum would end up serving as a footstool for dump cats and seagulls.

At McDonald's Home Hardware in town, my smiling friend Dennis was happy to hook me up with a new vacuum. I can't think of a major appliance that Dennis has not been able to provide over the years. He has delivered everything from lawnmowers to washing machines, always smiling, just like his dad before him.

I drove the new vacuum home myself and unpacked it. It had a few more bells and whistles than my first one, including an ergonomically correct handle and an exhaust filter. It was shiny. It was green.

Still, I felt hugely ambivalent about it. My inner child looked at it, shrugged and walked away. But I knew it meant something and I finally figured it out. Middle age.

THE TALIBAN MINK

The mink first struck in broad daylight. A pen full of guinea fowl began screaming and flapping and I rushed over to see a bird struggling in the corner with something that looked like the collar of a coat my mother once had. I shouted and the mink turned to examine me. It had a small face and bright beady eyes, but what struck me most was the blood on his open lips and what looked like a feral grin. When I shouted and reached for the pen door, the mink shot through a small hole in a rotted board at the back of the pen.

The bird was injured, limping and bleeding from the neck. I ran to the house for my medical kit. By the time I got back, the injured guinea was dead. The mink had returned to kill it and was in the process of trying to pull the carcass through the tiny hole. Interrupted again, the mink offered a look of irritation before it fled. I should have brought my gun.

I spent the whole afternoon inspecting the fowl pens, blocking holes here and there and rattling doors. I thought

I had done a good job. Some reading on the lifestyle of mink indicated that they are wily creatures that will kill for killing's sake, unlike weasels that kill to eat. Mink have a blood lust.

Sure enough, the next morning the entire pen of nine guinea fowl was dead. None were eaten though, just gnawed briefly at the neck. The mink had found a small space between a wall and the roof and squeezed through. Apparently, if a mink can get its head through a space, its body follows like smoke up a chimney.

I will confess that I never liked the guinea fowl much. When they were free ranging as yard birds, they screamed all day long. Once one hen shouted their cry of *Buck Wheat, Buck Wheat*, they were off in a chorus. If they roosted in the barn, it always seemed to me that they deliberately sat above the sheep's water bowls and feeders, which they contaminated at will. When I tried chasing them away, they would flee outside and fly up to roost on the roof of the house and cackle at me. They drove one plumber to distraction by hooting and hollering at him all day long while he worked in the barn.

But the sight of the slain guineas reminded me of the good times. The way they would nest furtively, outdoors in a patch of long grasses or brush, clinging to their eggs in the foulest of weather. It was nearly impossible to catch the resulting guinea chicks. Long before they could fly, they learned to run and then stop suddenly and cling to the ground silently, just as their mother had done when they were eggs.

The only way to lure guineas into a pen was to scatter kernels of corn. They could not resist corn. I had used that technique to corral them into the pen where they now lay dead. I collected their carcasses in feedbags, marvelling at their spotted black-and-white feathers, and missing their imperious squawking heads.

The pen beside the guineas' was almost identical in structure — wooden walls with two steel-mesh walls topped with green steel roofing. A corner pen, it housed a red-golden pheasant and a trio of pheasant hens. These were "new" birds, replacements for Mao and the Mrs. who had lived long and fruitful lives. I bought them at a bird fair, where all manner of fowl and rabbit were sold. The cock bird pheasant was at least two years old and in full and glorious feather. The hens, small and shy, were plain brown with mere tints of the gold that fringed the male's neck. I examined their pen from all angles. It looked secure and fine, complete with a skylight covered in two-inch steel mesh and a small ornamental spruce tree for them to use as cover when they were not perching.

As I closed the pen door, I caught sight of the mink again. He lunged at the steel mesh in the far corner of the pheasant pen. Leaping in the air, he rattled his furry mink claws on the steel. Then he fled, before Wally the Wonder Dog rounded the corner like a heat-seeking missile. Fast and furtive, the mink was. He disappeared beneath the barn into an elaborate series of tunnels and caves he had built there. This was his base of operations — the place where he would stockpile any food he could drag into the depths.

The next morning was another battle scene from hell. The pheasants had been slaughtered in the night. I had only known them for a month, and they were just beginning to relax in their new home and nod curiously when they saw me bringing them fresh water and food. Now they were gone, their beauty wasted. The brilliant red, green and golden feathers of the cock pheasant's cape blew around the silent pen. I cursed the mink, imagining the searing fear the birds must have had when they saw it swinging its lithe body through the two-inch steel mesh on the skylight. It left a smudge of blood when making its escape.

Two pens of banty chickens and one pen of Silver Sussex chickens were all that remained. The banty pens were solid steel mesh, including the floor of the pens, which were covered over with wood chips and shavings. The little birds, red banty and white-and-black Rock Columbus, were nervous and flighty now. I had discovered the Columbus hens both had bad feet after I brought them home from the bird fair, so they had a smaller separate pen where I could reach them easily and try to repair the damaged limbs. They were matted together, rooster and hens, in a fearful bundle of feathers in the nesting box. And the red banties, who had been a part of a petting zoo before I got them, cowered nervously and danced away to the farthest corner of their pen. Before this they had never shown any fear, even turning so bold as to peck at Wally's loopy bull terrier nose when he sniffed at them. Now they had witnessed the execution of their neighbours, and they had good reason to be afraid.

The Silver Sussex were Moose's chickens. Although he had never been disposed to birds before, when he saw the magnificent white rooster with a cape of lacy black feathers around his neck and a handsome, five-point red comb above fleshy wattles, Moose was chicken-smitten. Silver Sussex are a rare breed of chicken these days, although they were once as standard an issue of chicken as the Barred Rock on most farms throughout North America, performing the dual function of providing meat and eggs. Specialization and factory farming had rendered them little more than a curiosity, but Moose thought that such beauties should be preserved. He had high hopes of hatching eggs in the spring and maintaining a small lovely flock. Six hens shared the pen, dubbed the "skyscraper" because it was a good storey-and-a-half tall and filled with perches at various heights.

How glorious it had been to come home from the bird fair and put the varied fowl into their new homes. When the next morning dawned, their crowing filled the air — a cacophony of three tenor voices set at various volumes. By far the loudest was the big Silver Sussex. Moose called him Foghorn Leghorn, and we rushed down that first morning to watch the rooster fill himself up with air and *cock-a-doodle-doo* so hard that he had to sit back on the heels of his craggy white feet to avoid falling over backwards.

Moose made a special point of turning the Silver Sussex pen into a fortress to ward off the cutthroat mink. Steel siding went up and $100 worth of steel mesh wrapped the pen. We stapled and nailed until night fell.

Alas, there was no crowing in the morning. I looked out the bedroom window and saw yet another massacre; the Silver Sussex were scattered like ripped feather pillows on the floor of their pen. The mink must have made an aerial attack on Foghorn and crew, scaling the walls of the pen and squeaking through a small gap in the rafters. We cried desperate tears, while the banties hid their heads beneath their wings. From the sniffing Wally was doing around their pen, it was evident that the mink had tried and failed to kill them, too.

As unfortunate as the events in the chicken pens were, at the same time carnage of a different sort was going on in the world at large. Three weeks before the arrival of the mink, the World Trade Center Twin Towers and the Pentagon had been struck by terrorists in hijacked airliners. In our microcosm, we responded exactly as the Americans did. We declared all-out war on the "Taliban Mink."

Shooting the mink was not going to be feasible, unless he happened to appear on open ground, but even then mink are fast. Poison was also out of the question since Wally would surely find it before the mink did. The only solution seemed to be a trap.

Off we went to the farm supply store, where we found a mink-sized, Hav-A-Hart humane trap. Rectangular and squat, the steel-metal-piped trap had entrances on either end that led to a platform in the middle where bait could be placed. One step too close to the bait triggered the closing of gates and the offending animal would be trapped — or the offending hand, as mine was judged to be several times.

Obviously, the Taliban Mink was fond of raw chicken; however, a fine pink chicken wing left in the Hav-A-Hart did not entice him. Alone and out of my depth, I turned to the Internet for advice, signing onto a listserv of chicken enthusiasts called Chickens 101. The word "mink" sent chills through the chat group, where normal topics of conversation tend towards discussing cute names for your chickens and ways to conceal chicken pets from downtown landlords. When it came down to a serious question involving the life and death of chickens, the suggestions flew fast and furious. Stinky, canned, seafood cat food, the more offensive the better, was the bait recommended by someone who had tangled with a weasel in his henhouse. This made sense, since mink like to live near water where they can eat small fish and frogs. Peanut butter, chunky not smooth, was also highly recommended. A woman in Northern Illinois swore by sunflower seeds. She claimed to have live-trapped sixteen raccoons, five possums and one groundhog using nothing but sunflower seeds.

I tried all of those tricks and any others I could think of to tempt the mink into the trap, but nothing worked. Instead, the mink focused his efforts on trying to find a weak link in the cage containing the surviving banties. Every morning, Wally the Wonder Dog sniffed every inch of the perimeter of the pen for traces of mink. One day I watched him trail off from the pen, following the scent of the mink into the pasture field and down to the pond.

Winter was beginning to set in and the pond water was icy cold. Wally paid no attention to me and focused on the smell of the mink as it curved around tree stumps and wound its way to the water's edge. I have seen Wally track wild animals before. His nose becomes a dedicated instrument. He was foiled when the scent ended at the water's edge.

In the case of his usual prey, the groundhog, Wally's ritual is to "give them notice" when he fails to catch them. He does this by voiding his bowels in their holes. It becomes a morning ritual for him to make the rounds of the groundhog-infested field and leave his constitutional calling card on their doorsteps. This would certainly encourage me to find new lodgings were I a groundhog and I have always thought of it as "fair warning."

There was no sign of a mink hole or a den, so I watched as Wally waded into the freezing pond water and pooped on some grassy reeds just below the surface. That was his Declaration of War.

Stymied, we called in outside forces. Mike the Local Trapper of legendary proportion was convinced that what we needed was a leghold trap. However, a quick check around the neighbourhood revealed that every leghold trap was in use. This led me to believe that the entire township was in a state of fur-coated siege. Although he had never trapped a mink, Mike suggested alternatives and rigged up a noose trap in the tiny opening to the mink's first killing pen. Mink are curious creatures, explained Mike. If they think there is something within their grasp to kill, they will try. The tiny noose had a disturbing, primitive quality. I imagined the mink speeding through it like Wile E. Coyote in the *Road Runner* cartoons and being suddenly "hung up."

I took an old, white banty hen from the safe pen and put her in an old, steel-wire birdcage I had bought at an auction long ago. Then I hung the birdcage from a piece of chain-link more suited to hauling logs than hanging birdcages. The hen was secure enough, although I feared for her psyche.

The mink took a look that night, but, smart mink that he was, he simply swept the noose trap aside. No doubt he rattled the birdcage, but the banty hen was well secured.

Long days and nights of battling the Taliban Mink were wearying. Occasionally, a red-golden feather would turn up in the grass or I would find a white-and-black Silver Sussex feather on a bale of straw. The surviving banty roosters seemed to fear to crow, and without the incessant call of the guinea fowl, an ominous silence fell over the farm. Every time I walked to the barn, I imagined the Taliban Mink peering at me from his low-level cave underneath the barn, plotting his little mink plots.

And then one day it struck me. The mink had been successful because he knew what we were thinking. He knew that we thought we had created impenetrable pens, but he knew enough to find their flaws. He knew that a trap was a trap and he distrusted anything strange. He was just waiting for us to make one little mistake that would allow him to get at the remaining chickens. We were human — he knew a mistake was just a matter of time.

That's when I decided to turn the tables and think like a mink.

The mink enjoyed live prey and the fury of the chase. The more fearful the birds — the more they screeched and bounced off the walls — the better. Although the Hav-A-Hart trap had been a bust, its premise struck me as reasonable. The problem was luring the mink into the trap. The only lure strong enough would be the promise of a kill. I turned to the old white hen and pronounced her the One, the lonely unicorn, the goat tied to a tree, the sacrificial lamb — unless I could help it.

Moose helped me raise and wire the Hav-A-Hart trap so that its entrance was fixed over a mousehole-sized opening in one of the killing pens. All other avenues of entry were blocked with wire or filled in with insulation foam. If the mink wanted the chicken, the only access route was through the trap.

I felt bad leaving the small white chicken in the big pen that still bore spatters of blood from the fallen guinea fowl. She had a bed of cedar shavings and straw, and I added a bowl of torn lettuce next to her grain, fervently hoping that she was not having her last supper.

Two nights passed uneventfully, but came the dawning of the third morning the banty rooster was crowing. We ran out to the pen and, sure enough, the Taliban Mink was spitting and hissing from the tightly locked Hav-A-Hart trap, while the unharmed hen quivered with her head under her wing in the cedar shavings. There was a terrible smell in the pen — the musky odour of a fearful mink. Wally began dancing and barking and the mink hissed, expelling a stream of air through its incredibly sharp little fangs. Then the air filled with a high sharp scream and we all jumped back. The mink tossed its head fitfully and began biting the steel bars, clutching them with his handy brown paws and pulling with all of his strength.

The cage was placed on a picnic table where we watched the mink. Much about it was rat-like and bright-eyed, but the length of its body added lively movement and a dart of urgency to each gesture. It was smaller than my forearm, making the savagery of its killing all the more difficult to comprehend.

All throughout the process, Moose had been dealing with Faye and Joe, our animal-loving West Coast friends, who pleaded leniency for the mink. But this was not a creature that could become domesticated, or change its lifestyle, or begin to comprehend our concept of "the error of its ways."

Nor, I fear, could it have been relocated without presenting a danger to some other farmer's fowl. My new-found cyber-friends at Chickens 101 were loudly asserting that they did not want that mink dropped off anywhere near their coops. Unfortunately for the mink, our two competing lifestyles had overlapped and I had won. Moose dispatched the mink with a quick bullet in the brain. It would never hold brilliant feathers in its mouth again.

Capturing a mink is no mean feat. I stared at its inert body in the steel cage and drew it out to have a look. The fur was soft, not silky the way we think of fur, but there were layers to it. The head was small, almost bat-like, with tiny ears. The teeth were tiny perfect daggers.

"I don't know what you are thinking, but you couldn't even make a headband out of it," warned Moose.

No, I was not thinking about a headband, or even a fur collar, but something about the trauma of the experience made me want to preserve the moment in some way. I decided I would skin the mink and keep its pelt as a reminder to always be watchful for predators.

I have cleaned fish, eviscerated chickens and supervised the butchering of lambs, but removing the hide of an elongated rodent was an opportunity that had never presented itself. A quick run through the talents of my various friends assured me that none of them were likely to offer

much in the way of advice. I knew it should not be difficult but, as with any such crafty endeavour, there had to
be some techniques that were better than others. So I did
what every modern farmer does these days, I searched
the Internet.

I have become fairly handy at using this computer
tool. At least, if you make a mistake on it, no one needs
to know and you can start again. You can run into brick
walls of information, but you can't injure yourself the
way you can with a hammer or a drill.

I am not sure exactly what search words I used, but
after visiting a number of web sites that encouraged me
to send the mink to them for stuffing along with a big fat
cheque, I finally found a site run by a 15-year-old from
North Carolina whose hobby is skinning rodents and
roadkills. Young, home-schooled Amy had photo-docu-
mented the step-by-step skinning of a rat. It was graphic,
but virtually bloodless, and I figured if a 15-year-old
could do it, I could at least try.

Amy had all sorts of tools and scalpels and special
scissors. I decided I would have to get by with an X-Acto
knife, kitchen shears and a set of pliers. I assembled my
tools on the picnic table and positioned the mink tummy-
side up on a wooden board covered with newspaper.

Although her instructions were quite clear, Amy's
web site did not print out properly, so I kept having to
ask Moose to go back into the house to check to see if I
was doing things correctly and to find out what came
next. Between Moose and Amy, I navigated the skinning
of the mink and avoided the dread anal sacs that could
have doomed the project if they had been nicked. It was

work that took patience and a certain willingness to look closely at that which we do not normally even think closely about. Pulling the tailbones out of the tail of a furred animal using needle-nose pliers while seated at a picnic table is an almost surreal experience. The pelt rolled up over the head of the mink just like a tight sock, once the legs had been clipped free. When it was over, I had a full pelt with four little paws. It even had the original ears. We stretched it on the board and rubbed the skin side with salt to begin the tanning process. I felt a strange sort of catharsis, but the white chicken kept her head tightly under her wing for days.

An announcement was spread throughout the land about the apprehension of the Taliban Mink by Special Operations Forces Code Name "Vengeance Most Fowl," who reported the beast had been rendered spineless. It was another one of those days written in infamy.

I expect the story will become twisted as it spreads in the telling. The body count will rise and the neighbours will add their own tales of murderous creatures and attacks from the wild. My chickens are safe now and, ultimately, I will become the subject of great envy. After all, how many farmwomen do you know who have a mink's coat hanging in their barn?

OSAMA BIN CLUCKIN MEETS HIS MATCH

There are not many folks who go around trying to buy chickens at the outset of the Canadian winter. There is a good reason for this. Chickens tend to stop laying eggs as the days get shorter, although since the days get colder, they also continue to require the same sort of pricey feed as though they were laying eggs. Of course, one can insulate the chicken barn and install automatic lighting systems to confuse the chickens into thinking they are living in Palm Beach during July, but when you stack the cost of doing that beside the price of a dozen eggs, it just does not bear further discussion.

Still, after losing Moose's favourite chickens to the Taliban Mink, it occurred to me that a gift of chickens might be just the thing to raise the spirits of the whole barnyard. I called the breeder of the rare Silver Sussex chickens upon which the mink had committed genocide and told him my sad tale of woe. Now, it would be fairly easy for a chicken breeder to hang up the phone on a woman who said that a mink had killed all the birds she bought a few weeks earlier, so she would like to get some more, if you please. But I made a point of explaining that they were actually Moose's chickens and he had cared for them as though he had hatched them himself. We had vanquished the mink and had a totally secure, steel-coated pen in which to house the new birds. The clincher was saying that we missed the hearty morning crow of a Silver Sussex. Chicken fanciers all understand the importance of hearing that morning crow.

Dave the Chicken Man consulted with his wife and they agreed that he had quite enough Silver Sussex and assorted other exotic birds, so he could supply me with a rooster and three hens. I was ecstatic.

Moose prepared the pen for his new birds. They would share the secure space occupied by the red banties. It was partially divided by plywood and we installed heavy-gauge, one-inch plastic mesh to divide the remainder. When we released the big chickens into their new pen, the little banties flew up to their roost and watched the giant white fellows peck their way around the pen.

The next morning there was crowing at dawn. The Silver Sussex rooster had a blustery tenor and the red banty rooster followed his lead with a rapid-fire but lyrical burst of notes. We lay in bed listening and smiling.

Then the crowing stopped. Suddenly. We waited. Silence. When roosters are in crowing mode, they do not reach a crescendo and just stop. We leapt from the bed, sending duvet and dog flying while the theme from the movie *Jaws* played in our heads, calling up visions of *Taliban Mink — The Sequel*.

The pen was a bloody mess and both roosters were wearing red. It seems that in the excitement of their first crowing duet, they had declared war on each other through the plastic mesh dividing their pen. It appeared as though the Sussex had grabbed the banty by the neck and tried to pull him through to the other side. His cheek was torn in a jagged rip, while the Sussex rooster had no broken skin. In typical chicken fashion, the banty hens had circled the bloodied rooster and were starting to peck at him. He was groggy and unsteady, a punch-drunk rooster. The Taliban Mink had been vanquished, but it now seemed we had a new terrorist on our hands. By his actions, the Sussex rooster had named himself "Osama bin Cluckin" and the vicious hens on the attack became the "Al-Qaeda Girls' Club."

We removed the injured bird to the kitchen for assessment and repairs, all the while cursing the big rooster for turning mean and hurting the little guy. I washed his battered beak and carefully cleansed his wound. Stitches were out of the question, so I simply dressed it with the all-purpose wound ointment I use on the dog.

The rooster was not a well-looking chicken. He kept his head bowed and rocked unsteadily on his feet in the birdcage we set up for him in the parlor. Even a tantalizing salad of shredded lettuce, carrots and spinach failed to interest him. I went to bed thinking that by morning I might be looking for a new banty rooster.

Instead, I awoke to crowing inside and outside the house. The banty crowed all morning, which made interesting background music when I received the unsolicited call from the rug cleaning company soliciting my business.

"No, I do not want my rug cleaned. Why would I? Listen to this, can't you tell I live in a barn?" A banty rooster crow directly into the receiver of a telephone must pack a certain wallop because I have never heard from this exceptionally persistent firm again.

After a few days in the house, the rooster was ready to return to his hens. The large gauge plastic mesh between the two pens had been replaced with the same steel mesh that thwarted the Taliban Mink. There would be no repeat performance.

Osama bin Cluckin perked right up when he saw the little red bird being dropped in the pen. He strutted forward, making the trilling kind of growl roosters can make in anticipation of something happening. Then he stopped. The red banty's head cocked to one side and in an instant he was in the air, propelling himself feet forward into the steel mesh. He was flapping madly. When his claws bounced off the steel, the cocky little fellow did an angry strut and flew at the steel mesh again. All this time, Osama was standing perfectly still, eyeing the antics of the bird one-sixth his size with what appeared to be chicken bemusement.

One tends to assume that the big guy always picks on the little guy, but in the world of chickens this does not hold true. Just as sure as there is a Chihuahua out there who is willing to take on a Great Dane and a Shetland pony who refuses to yield to a Clydesdale, there are banty roosters who believe that it is their mission in life to vanquish fellow-fowl that could crush them with a drumstick.

In keeping with his freshly revealed personality disorder, we named the little banty Ayatollah Crowmeiny.

When the days grow longer and spring grows closer, I will set up the incubator and begin collecting eggs from all of the hens. You can store eggs for several days in a cool dark place and they will remain vital, provided they are not shaken. Once I have a suitable number, I will begin the process of warming the eggs of the war-torn poultry factions. Little eggs or big eggs, they will all hatch within a day or so of each other. One can only wonder what sort of fluffy little terrorists they will be.

WALLY BALLYS

The words "Wally" and "ball" are frequently spoken in close proximity in my house.

Like terriers of any sort and like retrievers and dogs that chase birds, even like police dogs and drug-sniffing dogs, and just about every mutt you ever met — Wally the Wonder Dog has a thing about balls. He loves them. He wants to be near them; to touch them; to feel them. The sound of one ball bouncing is like a symphonic cymbal to him.

Sometimes he only wants to smell a ball and nudge it with his nose to see how far it will roll. He enjoys doing this on the Mexican-tile floor in the farm kitchen — bumping a ball into a grouted groove and seeing if it will follow a pattern, sort of like playing pinball in slow motion on a mammoth surface.

Outdoors, Wally plays his own version of soccer. He heads the ball off his huge nose and works it nimbly with his front paws. When a human is the "kicker" Wally expects a good firm kick, one that he can chase down and run back, arching his neck as he propels the soccer ball along the grass.

People who visit the farm, be they census takers or clever sleuths who have found me out, end up spending more time watching Wally play with his balls than they do asking me questions. If I give him a small grain pail, he runs around furiously scooping up every ball in the yard and prancing around with his balls in a pail.

Those of us who deal with ball-loving dogs also deal with the cost of balls. The care, feeding and maintenance of companion animals is a huge industry, and I suspect if it were analyzed in detail a good percentage of the funds spent on "toys" would be devoted to round items of various sizes and textures.

Wally has deconstructed many valuable soccer balls and volley balls in his day, So he is now trained to understand that he must have a hard rubber Kong toy or some other form of indestructible mouthguard in his mouth before he can begin manipulating other balls.

I tested more than 100 balls before I found one that served this purpose and proved entertaining. I could not pass a sporting goods store without checking out the ball section. I made a beeline for the toy section of every pet store I passed, looking for new balls. I haunted the booths at dog shows, hoping that something new would show up.

Then one day I found a hard rubber ball at Canadian Tire. It was covered in dust, but you could see that it was supposed to be white. It was a lacrosse ball. I will try any ball once.

Wally loved it. He loved the smell and touch of it. The size was right and it was neither too heavy, nor too light. Moose threw it down the laneway and it bounced spectacularly, even erratically. Still, I must tell you that there is nothing that looks stupider than a Canadian trying to find a white ball in a snowdrift.

The Canadian Tire lacrosse ball lasted about two weeks before it began to crumble. I was discouraged, but after all, it did come from the store Canadians know and love as "Crappy Tire." I figured that there had to be a higher quality lacrosse ball out there somewhere.

After trying all sorts of mail-order lacrosse balls, I finally found the brand of my dreams in a sporting goods store just down the road from the farm. It was smooth and solid and very white, but Wally could not put a dent in it.

When I went back to the store to order a carton of the balls, I discovered to my great joy that they were also available in cheerful bright shades of blue, orange and yellow. Yes!

People who have ball-obsessed dogs can understand the significance of my discovery. Dogs who love balls are fixated on the things. That lovable Jack Russell terrier on the television sitcom *Frazier* was so focused on tennis balls that he had to have at least four root canals performed because he wore his teeth down on the balls. At least Indian rubber absorbs some of the pressure and a tooth can't get stuck inside.

Wally was overjoyed with his new balls. I decided to test them out on other dogs. A neighbour's rangy mutt loved the ball so much that he buried it and we never found it again. The balls seemed to suit everything from miniature dachshunds to Labrador retrievers. However,

I knew the true test would be to expose the ball to other bull terriers.

Through the miracle of e-mail I had accumulated quite a number of friends who are owned by bull terriers. I decided to ask a select group of them to "test" Wally Ballys. They came from all over North America — dogs with names like Rocky and Tyson and "The Kelvinator." I sent out sample balls with instructions to destroy at will. Then I waited.

The balls were a success. If they had a flaw it was that the dogs could not destroy them and at least one bull-headed test bully decided that it was not interesting to play with something he failed to rent asunder. One test owner reported that she had tried to stab a ball with a steak knife and she couldn't put a dint in it. Just the sort of thing a dog might think of doing, I suppose. My friend Shari even created a Wally Bally game, tying two balls in a sock and letting her ball-crazed bitches, Maddy and Maizey, play by themselves. My testers were willing to testify to the soundness of the balls and share the knowledge with their networks of doggy friends. I contacted the distributor and requested wholesale consideration to sell the balls to dog lovers. Thus, I became a middle-woman and an entrepreneur of balls.

"Wally Ballys" burst on the dog world scene at Silverwood, the largest dog show in North America devoted only to bull terriers. I had two dozen balls in every colour to display in an elegant clear glass vase. Adorning the balls were stickers of my own design featuring Wally holding a ball in his mouth. It took many attempts to come up with the design, and, by the time I did, it was too late for the printer to order them as pre-made, round stickers. They were printed in haste as a great favour, and I cut each one out by hand with manicure scissors on the long drive to Silverwood, deep in the heart of America.

Try to imagine a dog show on Mars, because that is exactly what Silverwood turned out to be. The Sheraton Hotel in Mars, Pennsylvania, was the host venue and hundreds of bull terriers from across North American showed up, arriving in all manner of vehicle accompanied by owners, handlers, groomers, grooming tables, groom-ing boxes, dog crates, dog beds and, of course, every toy known to dogdom.

"Welcome to Mars," said the check-in clerk. I smiled, weakly. There was a bowl of dog biscuits on the counter. Wally gobbled one and let out a great burp.

Bull terriers were everywhere. Pure white ones, ones with eye patches, chestnut-red ones, black ones with white trim and striped, brindle ones, like Wally. Some were dainty mini-bull terriers, while others bore the bulk that gives bull terriers the nickname: Pig dogs.

The bellman was full of questions as we made our way up in the elevator.

"These are the Budweiser beer 'Spuds' dogs, right? Like the kind that General Patton had? Funny looking, or am I not supposed to say that?" Wally licked his knees.

I was sharing booth space with a woman from Cal-gary who I had never met, but we had shared plenty of e-mail letters. Moose was nervous. He thinks the people you meet by e-mail could turn out to be crackpots or serial killers. Marty Schacht turned out to be a nicely rounded, middle-aged woman, who just happened to be travelling with two huge trunks full of bull terrier "stuff" ranging from leashes and collars with bullys on them to note cards and sculptures of bull terriers surfing and riding motorcycles. Moose still thought he was right, until we sat down at dinner and the two of them became so engrossed talking about their dogs that I could not get a word in edgewise.

The next day, Wally and I hit the booth first thing in the morning and set up our wares. The place was jammed with people and every one of them was wearing something with a bull terrier on it.

The excitement was far too much for Wally, who yowled every time a customer walked away with a Wally Bally. Dipping into the inventory, I gave him an orange Wally Bally to play with. He promptly dropped it and ended up chasing it under the table next to ours which featured hand-painted glass bull terrier items. Talk about a bully in a china shop. I wanted another mug without a handle any way.

Quite a number of dogs left Silverwood with Wally Ballys in their toy bag. One cannot describe the joy a Canadian feels receiving payment in U.S. funds for goods purchased in Canadian funds. Naturally, I invested my profits in all manner of merchandise covered with bull terriers.

Since then, Marty has allowed me to sell "virtually indestructible" Wally Ballys through her Internet bull terrier shopping mall, where a percentage of all sales are donated to organizations that find new homes for bull terriers that have been abused or abandoned. So Wally Ballys went international — I have had orders from England, Hawaii and Australia. My best customer is an American dog named Roy, who has a grand total of 30 blue Wally Ballys. At last, I acquired professional-looking labels and I devised a clever way of packaging the balls in tubes made out of blue file folders. Once or twice a week I show up at the post office and confound the post-mistress with my rolling stock.

Wally is not impressed by my entrepreneurial venture. I have to store "the product" on a shelf well away from his reach or he claims it as his own. It is impossible to do any packaging when he is in the room without having him shoplift at least one sales unit. I once left him alone in the truck with a bag full of blue tubes I intended to mail and he chewed three of them open in the time it takes to return a movie rental. No matter how you look at it, it's a dog-eat-ball world out there.

THE EASY CHRISTMAS TREE ROUTE

Getting a fresh-cut Christmas tree is quite convenient when you just have to take a few steps off the front porch to find one. That is what I have taken to doing, thanks to my own mistakes.

Planting trees is an annual ritual on the farm. I enjoy planting little trees that look like nothing at all for many years. Then, 10 years down the road, there seems to be a cluster of beautiful trees that sprang from nowhere.

There is something wonderful in that moment, and it takes you back to the day that the trees were planted. The great selective capacity of memory may recall the weather that day, or details of your wardrobe or the seed you were planting in the garden. In fact, I remember that I was wearing a red plaid shirt and denim shorts on the late May day when I planted the blue spruce trees at the edge of the garden. Beside them, I planted mounds of squash plants, and the little trees had disappeared in the vines by August.

The blue spruce barely looked like trees at all. They were just singular pokey branches, with straggly damp roots. I started out with eight of them and six survived the first winter. Four were near the house and two down at the end of the laneway. They were slow-growing trees and I seldom paid them any attention. I also planted half a dozen dwarf apple trees right next to some of them without really thinking about what I was doing.

Fifteen years later, the four blue spruce that I had planted eight feet apart were towering over the dwarf apples and their branches were growing thickly together. If they were not thinned, the apple trees would receive no sunlight and the spruce trees would become a wall with strangling roots. It was not going to be a pretty sight.

The time had come to take the easy Christmas tree route and thin the orchard evergreens in the process. Blue spruce are beautiful trees and they are notoriously expensive at commercial lots. The selected tree came from the middle of the planting. I thought it would be smaller than our Christmas tree usually is, but when it was laid out on the front lawn it measured 16 feet. A good 2 feet had to be trimmed so that it would fit the high ceiling of the family room.

It was sometime around the measuring of the tree and the start of an afternoon snowfall that Moose and I gave each other the same funny look. Every year for two decades we had taken the huge Christmas tree into the house through the family-room windows at the back of the house. They were big cottage-style windows that popped right out. It was always a challenge to get the tree upright, something that tended to involve levers and at least one person resting the whole tree on their back while the other figured out what to do next.

However, this year, there were no cottage-style windows in the back room. After two decades of cursing those windows for allowing winter winds to whistle straight through them, we had replaced the whole lot with fine and dandy, newfangled thermal pane windows. Those windows were not going to pop out anywhere, and they would only slide halfway open. This is the sort of realization that causes one's lower lip to protrude while one's forehead wrinkles.

The tree was also bushy. While branches could be removed on the side that would be against the wall, the rest of the tree had a very full skirt. Our first thought was to try to tie the branches close to the sides by wrapping the tree round and round with a long nylon rope. That did not work. Then we considered cutting the tree back to more than half its size so that it would fit through a half-opened window. That didn't seem in keeping with the *esprit de Noël* we had ardently established over the decades. As long as there was room in the house for a great big hunk of nature to be swathed in lights and ornaments and candy canes, we wanted to fill the room with it.

A plan was formulated. Actually, more a plan of attack. Moose was sure that if we got part of the tree into the house, the rest would be sure to follow. If we re-arranged certain elements of the foyer and the kitchen, he thought we could stuff the tree through them and down the hallway to the family room. The important thing, he said, was to just keep it moving and not look back.

Even somewhat trimmed, the big tree was heavy. Blue spruce are also prickly trees and their short needles can penetrate mittens. Moose led the charge, pulling the base of the tree up the front steps and through the door. The boot tray was the first victim, and I tripped over two unmatched Wellington boots while pushing my end of the tree through the foyer.

In the kitchen, tables and chairs had been shifted but we had not considered things like the hanging wineglass rack beside the door and the sugar bowl on the kitchen counter. Fortunately, the forward motion of the tree held everything against the wall. The corridor was the biggest problem since the tree filled it totally. I pushed, Moose pulled and somehow we made it to the family room. Getting the tree upright was the usual chore, but it was finally in place and a wire around the middle ensured that it was not going to fall over. I retrieved two wineglasses and a dishtowel from inside the tree.

Decorating the blue spruce was an exercise in scratching. The pointed needles were hard on the fingers and forearms. I found myself wearing long sleeves and leather gloves. Of course, in the end it was "the best tree ever," just as every Christmas tree should be.

The next day I walked down to the mailbox through powdery knee-high snow. It was a perfect winter morning: crisp and still with everything, except the cardinals at the bird feeder, appearing in some shade of white, black or silver, while the evergreens bowed roundly under a coat of snow. Wally the Wonder Dog chose to plow his way through the snow, pausing to bury his face in it all the way to the ground to sniff whatever it is that dogs can sniff in the snow. All seemed sparkling and right with the world.

The road had been cleared and Len the Mailman was able to deliver right on time. I stuffed the mail in my big jacket pocket and headed back up the lane. That's when I noticed the two blue spruce trees at the end of the lane. Or rather, the one-and-a-half blue spruce trees at the end of the laneway. The snow had covered whatever tracks there might have been but the evidence was far from circumstantial. The top half of one tree had been sawed off, leaving a base about six feet high. Whoever did it was either very tall or they had backed their truck up to the tree and worked from that vantage.

There are lots of trees in my part of the country, plenty for everyone. I have never turned anyone down when asked to cut a Christmas tree from my woods. So the taking of a tree that had obviously been deliberately planted at the end of a laneway was a malicious act of vandalism. Wally sniffed around it, but came up clueless.

I suppose I should have felt angry, but all I felt was saddened that someone in the community betrayed a certain trust. In fact, I had a small chuckle thinking of them trying to decorate their prickly prize. Commercial tree vendors in the area do not carry blue spruce because of the exorbitant price tag, so anyone having such a tree would become a mark of conversation. Although tempted to create a large sign saying something seasonally appropriate like "Merry Christmas Idiot," I decided to do nothing at all.

Of course, the neighbours had their own comments. Everyone thought it was "just terrible what this world is coming to."

At least, I now know where next year's tree is coming from. Early in the season, I plan to harvest the remaining blue spruce at the end of the lane for my own. It is a fine young tree and should fit right through the kitchen and the hallway without much trimming.

I really should have marked the blue spruce at the end of the laneway for Christmas harvesting some time ago. As nice an idea as it is, it seems that some idiot planted them directly below the hydro wires, which was bound to cause future complications.

Planting trees is a pastime that rewards itself over the years, but it helps to remember that a misplaced sapling can make a sap out of the most well-intentioned planter, even it if does make selecting a Christmas tree awfully easy.

SECRETS

I guess we all have secrets. Some of us keep them better than others. Some secrets are dark and painful, and some are as whimsical as the first crush of puppy love.

I don't have many secrets that haven't been told. But I do respect secrets and people who keep them.

When I was growing up, my mother used to always say, "We don't have any secrets in this house," which was her way of telling us that we could talk about anything and we should talk about anything — without fear of laughter or punishment.

So, it came as quite a surprise a few years ago when my father gathered the clan and declared that he had a secret — one he had kept for 50 years. A secret so big that he had never told a soul, not even my mother.

Now, my father is not the sort of man you would suspect of having a big secret. He was a dentist. A quiet man who poked around other people's mouths most of his life and who enjoyed a good game of golf and a gin martini. When he retired, he took up computers. Now he plays golf on his computer and drinks root beer. Secrets were never his style. He doesn't even like surprises.

Mom said she had no idea what he was on about. All she knew was that he had been typing on his computer for months.

The old boy played us out like kittens, until he finally heaved from his La-Z-Boy, and handed each of us identical packages.

"In there you will find the true story of what I did during the Second World War," he announced. It was his memoirs.

Well, that's all well and good, I thought. We all knew that Dad had been in the Army Dental Corps. Not much excitement there.

The only "war story" Dad ever enjoyed telling us was about his first glimpse of a certain Air Force dental assistant in training who had a particularly pleasing posterior. She was my mother, and they married three months after that first sighting.

Drawing himself to his full height, which seems to be shrinking with each passing year, Dad continued.

"As you know, I was denied the opportunity to serve overseas like your brave uncles. My childhood measles left me deaf in the right ear and that lousy ear spoiled my chances. So I sat out the war filling cavities for fighting men instead."

We all nodded politely.

Secretly, I always blessed that "lousy ear" for keeping my dad out of harm's way during the War.

I've read about the War and wars, and I've seen it all on TV and in the movies. I can't forget those images, and

I don't think we ever should. But I'm sure glad that my gentle, jovial father never had to face anything more brutal than a root canal.

Then Dad dropped the bomb.

"Well, that was just a cover," he said. "In actual fact, I was a secret agent working with British and Canadian Intelligence."

My dad was a spy!

That woke mother up.

As Dad explained it, when he was recruited by a Major in the British Secret Service he had to sign a document that bound him to the National Secrets Act for half a century. His own parents died not knowing what their son did during the war!

Images of James Bond whirled in our heads. No wonder he always liked his martini shaken, not stirred.

So, just what did you do, Dad?

Well, it all started with teeth. Dad and other secret agents in the Dental Corps would be shipped out to "secure" facilities, such as a chemistry lab at the University of Western Ontario, where they set up a field dental hospital and fixed the teeth of air-borne commandos, destined to be parachuted behind enemy lines on missions of espionage and other derring-do.

Then Dad became an information courier. While plans were being formulated for campaigns in Africa, Italy and Europe, my father was ferrying classified material to "safe houses" in various parts of Canada where war strategy was plotted based on Allied air-reconnaissance photos, information from the French and Dutch undergrounds, and even from German double agents.

Disguised as a Dental Corps Army private on leave, Dad casually carried secret documents in a well-worn haversack to avoid attention. At all times, he was accompanied by a special operations commando in civilian clothes, in case a Nazi operative tried to kill him.

Nazis in Canada! Nazi spies who could have killed my dad and absconded with war secrets!

And it got weirder. It seems that one of the reasons my father was red-flagged for secret agent duty was because of the 11 years he spent as a Boy Scout.

It was right there on page 8 in his book, where he detailed his education. Leadership and athletic accomplishments — including being an Eagle Scout with badges in everything from Navigation to Morse Code!

That was grounds to train my dad as a cryptic code specialist. We skimmed the pages where he talked about a computer named Colossus, the German code system known as Enigma, coded information labelled "Ultra," the planning of the invasion of Normandy.

At a secret base, messages were sent from British strategists in Canada to Bletchley Park in England — from my father direct to Winston Churchill's War Room.

I had the Dad from Intrepid.

Mom said, "I knew there was something fishy going on. You could have just told me."

"No, I couldn't," Dad said. And we kids agreed. Mother never could keep a secret. Heck, if she had known what Dad had been up to, we could have lost the war.

Dad's memoirs weren't just about secret missions. There were funny bits — things about bus trips, girls and Vera Lynn songs.

His fears had not been those of a combat soldier, they were the fears of imagining, of living with the anxiety of knowing about battles before they began. Terrible fears for a 22-year-old to live with, and then hold quietly for the next 50 years.

After Dad opened up to us about his secret war activity, he became downright chatty about it. He was a big hit at family reunions. In fact, he couldn't be left alone in a buffet lineup without word spreading from the salad bar to the roast beef that he had been a secret agent in the War.

When Dad and I finally had a long talk about his cloak and dagger memoirs, he asked me what I thought of his contribution to the war effort. And I told him I had been proud of him ever since the day we met Mr. Sullivan.

Dad had forgotten about Mr. Sullivan. We met him when I was about nine years old and we were crowded together in a lineup at the Canadian National Exhibition.

"Hey, Doc," a man called out to my dad. "You were the Army dentist, am I right?" My dad nodded, warily, no doubt concerned that he was going to hear some woeful story about wisdom teeth.

But Mr. Sullivan introduced himself in a most friendly manner.

"I always wanted to thank you for fixing my choppers before they sent me to France, Doc," he said, shaking my dad's hand. "I ended up in a German prisoner of war camp for three years, and if you hadn't fixed my teeth before I got there I could never have chewed my way through the stale bread and hard tack they gave us."

I had always believed that whatever my father did in the War it had to have made a difference. An army might march on its stomach, but first it had to be able to chew.

Secrets can be good things. Warm and sunny spots we visit within ourselves, but when you have to keep a secret that you are just bursting to tell, the only solace comes at the point of spillage.

The secret I kept from my dad all those years was that he'd always been my hero.

ALWAYS ON SUNDAY

It is almost a rule on my farm that any time an animal has a medical crisis it will occur on a weekend, most likely a holiday weekend when the sun is shining and any veterinarian in his right mind has gone fishing. At least as long as I am around, vets will be able to afford vacations.

Older animals can be surprisingly healthy one minute and flat on the ground the next, as I have found with my horses. At 28, old Lady's back is swaying and her rump seems bony, but she still winters in the open-sided shed and the out of doors. She and her 18-year-old daughter, Karma, are stout enough to rip and snort around the field. If a sheep gets in their way, they think nothing of picking it up by its woolly back and moving it. They are the palomino Queens of the barnyard and have known so few sick days that I could count them on their hooves.

So when I looked out of the upstairs window one wintry Sunday morning and saw old Lady laid flat in a snowbank, I went into emergency mode. She was down and her breathing was off. She would turn her head but she would not get up. I knew she heard me urging her, but she just moaned. She kicked at her belly in short jerks. I was terrified.

The vet arrived an hour later. In the interim, I managed to cajole the old girl to her feet. She was shaky, having been down for some time. I took her into the barn, and presented her with a warm bucket of molasses water. She wanted nothing, until I gave her an apple spiked with blue livestock salt. My neighbour "Hooter" Houston had told me that sometimes a horse will seem to present with colic when actually it needs fluids, and there is never any harm in getting fluids into an animal. Sure enough, after the salt, Lady drank the whole bucket of water. I brushed her, massaged her and sang cowboy songs to her. The moaning stopped, as did the kicking at her stomach. Her breathing became deep and regular and she nuzzled me for more apples. When the vet peered through the barn door, I had nothing to show him.

By virtue of appearing at the barn door, the vet had earned a fee, so he examined Lady and pronounced her old and well. That took about four minutes.

"Maybe I should float her teeth," he said.

So he got out his dental rasp and gently filed down any sharp back teeth that the old mare had. When that was done, Lady was ready to join her daughter in the field where they reared up together and ran bucking and farting around the yard, scattering sheep and generally acting like schoolkids on a snow day. The bill for that little adventure was worth about three months' food supply for both horses.

I cannot think of a serious health event involving a dog that has not occurred on a weekend. Porcupines must hide themselves carefully out of the reach of canines on weekdays.

Even the most innocent of actions can lead to an emergency trip to the vet. When Wally the Wonder Dog was a mere puppy, we were loading groceries into the truck on a Saturday afternoon when the little villain decided that he would try to jump out of the back window into the path of oncoming traffic. He had achieved launch mode when Moose reached up and managed to halt him in mid-air by grasping the upper portion of Wally's whip-like tail.

The puppy scream that resulted could have cracked concrete. This was followed by Wally-whirling-in-circles pain — a brindle dervish chasing his tail. Once confined in my arms, the little guy lay on his back, swaying his head, rolling his eyes and emitting pitiful squeals. Moose was distraught, although he had arguably prevented a total disaster.

We called the vet from the parking lot. It was closing time, but yes, the vet would stay behind to examine Wally's tail. We looked at the tail, but there was nothing to see. The top lay flat against his buttocks, while the tip curved up rather limply. As tails go, it was mighty forlorn.

Once he got to the vet's office, Wally's attitude improved greatly. He strolled around the waiting room chomping on every squeaky dog toy he could find and chasing the resident clinic cat to higher ground. But there was no wagging of the famously wagging tail.

Somehow, we managed to cajole Wally into holding still long enough for an x-ray. It revealed absolutely nothing, all bones in place, all bones aligned. What we had here was soft tissue damage and the cure involved doing absolutely nothing. The bill for that little escapade was worth about three months' food for all cats and dogs on the farm, including their gourmet cookies.

However, the *pièce de résistance* came one weekend in February during weather conditions that rivaled ice-floe collision season in Antarctica. Wally vomited on Friday. Considering some of the things he can get up to eating on a farm, this did not totally surprise me. From either end of him I have retrieved remarkable artifacts, including a rabbit's foot, the rubber hand of the stuffed monkey toy that I had kept since childhood and an assortment of lingerie items that would make Monica Lewinsky blush. The barnyard is also a sort of buffet of doggy snacks that certain companion animals seem to find irresistible — including sheep droppings and horse nuggets.

We decided to wait overnight to see if this was an isolated incident, but the following morning things had grown worse. Both ends of Wally were actively involved and he was a sad-looking fellow. Off to the vet.

I have always been fortunate to have caring and knowledgeable veterinarians. Dr. Kim is no exception. She is the kind of vet who will sit beside an animal, petting it and stroking it, while explaining what she thinks may ail it. Her hands rarely leave the subject of her attention. She was all over Wally that day. He had a temperature and the fact that he allowed it to be taken without protest was yet another bad sign. Blood was taken and antibiotics were started. We would get the results later in the evening and proceed from there.

In the meantime, I contacted Wally's breeder. One of the great pleasures and advantages of acquiring a dog from a breeder is having that person as a sort of backup support system and sounding board over all things concerning the dog. Heather listened carefully, as she has every time I have called her, including the first time — less than two hours after we had driven off with the puppy wrapped in a blanket. I think I was calling then to inquire if it was normal for bull terriers to have the hiccups. Being a breeder requires amazing patience as well as dedication.

Heather's concern was that young Rather's Wallace Stevens, like all bull terriers, was experiencing pain that he was not expressing and could be suffering from an intestinal blockage. The same consensus was reached when I dutifully presented Wally's symptoms to an Internet community of more than 600 red bull terrier lovers worldwide — check for a blockage and check fast. When the blood work returned with nothing extraordinary, we asked for a referral to one of the finest veterinary facilities in the world.

The Veterinary College at the University of Guelph in Southwestern Ontario is the Mayo Clinic of the animal world. When I studied sheep at the university, we were allowed to tour the large-animal clinic and marvel at the facilities for delicate surgeries on million-dollar racehorses and prize dairy cows. In another wing, the small-animal clinic caters to treating everything from house pets to champion breeding stock. We showed up first thing on Sunday morning with one sick puppy.

Wally needed fluids. He needed to be stabilized and he needed many tests. He was really sick. Moose had tears in his eyes when he noted that Wally had not even tried to lick the ears of any of the vets who had seen him. After slapping down a wad of cash and leaving a credit card imprint marked "sky's the limit," we watched hang-dog Wally shuffle down a corridor on a white-cloth leash with a blue-coated health team worker.

I remember leaving many dogs and cats at the vet's when I was a child. Lady, Blackie, Princess, Duchess, Winston and Charm, all had to stay overnight at the vet's and they never came back. We drove home wordless, utterly speechless — functional but non-responsive.

Over the following two days, Wally was the focus of intense medical attention. He had x-rays, a complete blood work panel, an ultrasound and an eco-cardiogram. Members of his veterinary team called to report on every procedure and they called morning, noon and night to provide details about his temperature and state of well-being. Once the vet even called just to say that Wally was taking an interest in playing with his ball. That was the only breakthrough Wally made in 48 hours; his temperature was still elevated. He was being fed intravenously. And, a slight heart murmur had been detected. The next step would be to open him up and take a look.

I am one of those who think of surgery as a last resort. Also, I have a slight heart murmur myself, and doctors are always cautious before sending me to an operating room. However, organic material such as sticks and bones does not necessarily show up in the tests Wally had been subjected to. I sent an e-mail to 600 bull terrier lovers around the world, asking for advice.

People may disguise themselves and lie and cheat and do stupid or silly things on the global coffee klatch

that is Internet chat, but one thing they take very seriously is the health of their pets. A long-time bull terrier
breeder, who had a great deal of experience with the
phenomenon of gastrointestinal blockages, suggested a
barium swallow for Wally. If there was something organic
clogging up his works the barium would locate it; if not,
we could rule out surgery, or "the zipper" as it is called
by those who are frequent visitors to the operating room.
Wally's barium swallow revealed no blockage, but it
saved him having stitches.

We went to see the boy that afternoon. I sat in a waiting room with other patients and their humans. It was
chemotherapy day and all of the dogs in the waiting room
were waiting for cancer treatment. One by one, technicians
came into the waiting room to greet each dog by name and
offer just the right sort of greeting, even if it meant getting
down on all fours to meet the dog on its own turf. I tried to
imagine a world in which humans were treated with such
compassion.

Wally was escorted from the elaborate intensive care
unit. He had eight feet of plastic tubing connecting his paw
to a rolling IV unit, but he still rallied to play soccer with
his ball. I looked into his eyes and saw mischief. He was
coming back.

Indeed, his temperature was getting closer to normal
and the vets had noticed a distinct change in attitude. He
had begun to lick the ears of his female technicians, and the
plan was to move him to a room next to intensive care,
since he had taken to barking when he wanted to play.

Two days later, we brought Wally home. No one
could explain what had gone wrong or why it had gone

right. He was almost exactly back to himself, except for the shaved belly which made him look quite punk. A few days later he was back to chasing squirrels and diving in snowdrifts.

The bill for that little adventure in "non-specific gastroenteritis" was enough to manage the whole farm, vehicles included, for three months.

Would I do it again? Well, of course, and always on a Sunday. That's the rule.

THIS LITTLE SQUIRREL BATTLES WINTER

When I sit at my office window in the second storey of the old yellow-brick farmhouse, all I can see are fields of white, dotted with the occasional cedar and a few gnarly old apple trees. And I see the tops of fence posts, with perhaps a single strand of page wire jutting above the snow line. The snow is that deep. It is folded over the landscape like a fluffy Hutterite duvet.

After a few years of mellow, even greenish winters, this deep snow business has left me feeling a bit like the proverbial squirrel who is late storing her nuts. Based on previous experience, I thought I had stocked enough firewood to keep the house warm well into 2003.

A huge old maple tree, with a stump so broad it could be carved into an armchair, had been rendered into firewood when its branches finally made it a peril. All summer long, I had been routinely loading chunks of maple into my blue wheelbarrow and stacking the wood outside or chucking it through a basement window. By late autumn, I had fourtenn cords of wood stacked beside the barn, along the fencerow and on the front porch. Another six cords were snuggled under the basement steps for easy access in foul weather.

A cord of wood — what we call a "face cord" — is four feet high and eight feet long. In a recent edition of *The New Yorker* magazine, I read that people living in lofts in Manhattan are paying $175 (US) for a single cord, but of course that includes delivery — and stacking.

Stacking is a kind of mental and physical exercise that combines a Zen-like attitude with the frustration inherent in assembling a Rubik's cube. Even when wood is cut in uniform lengths, it doesn't just fit together neatly without some consideration by the stacker. Sometimes it even falls down.

We who stack wood appreciate the intricacies of the process and regard it as something of an art form. We separate the fresh-cut "green" wood from the dried wood that shows cracks in the age rings, which will crackle when the wood burns. We treasure dried cedar that can be split into easy kindling wood that must be kept dry. We mix the size of logs, even the kinds of wood we incorporate into our woodpile – always trying for just the right mix. Even now, after 20 years of stacking, I still find myself admiring a well-stacked woodpile in someone else's yard or garage.

But there are winters in Wellington County, when the snowfall is massive. So massive that being woodstack proud means very little, because the wood stack is buried in snow. This winter, for instance, I can't even see the cords of wood that are stacked beside the fencerow.

That pile just happened to be close to the lane way, so along with the abnormal accumulations of snow, the wood is also buried under white stuff that has spewed relentlessly out of the snow blower in an effort to keep the lane clear.

Oops.

By New Year's, the front porch cords of wood I had stacked so precisely that they could have withstood the scrutiny of Martha Stewart were reduced to a few chunks and some limb wood.

My precious, dry and accessible basement wood supply is down to one emergency cord that I refuse to touch. Lest we forget the chaos an ice storm can bring. Even without hydro, wood can keep you warm and keep you cooking.

So I'm back to the famous blue wheelbarrow, digging out wood that is stacked beside the barn and wheeling it back to the house, where I stack it and let it dry all over again.

The sheep watch me with some amusement, before taking their daily exercise, which consists of tromping down a worn path through walls of snow three feet high until they reach their outdoor heated waterer, which remains blessfully unfrozen despite the weather.

I know that I could forego my wood exercise program and let the oil furnace do all of the work, but I like my developing biceps.

And in the end there is really something comforting about the heat of a wood fire, the crackling and the glow. The big old maple may be gone, but it's not forgotten, and this little squirrel isn't about to surrender to winter, yet.